# mike peyton's
# floating
# assets

**ADLARD COLES NAUTICAL**
LONDON

*Dedicated to John Barstow,*
*Tom Bolton and Jack Worsley,*
*who were lost on* Snipe *in 1963.*

Published by Adlard Coles Nautical
an imprint of A & C Black Publishers Ltd
36 Soho Square, London W1D 3QY
www.adlardcoles.com

Copyright © Mike Peyton 2008

First edition 2008

ISBN 978-0-7136-8935-8

A CIP catalogue record for this book is available from the British Library.

This book is produced using paper that is made from wood grown in managed, sustainable forests. It is natural, renewable and recyclable. The logging and manufacturing processes conform to the environmental regulations of the country of origin.

Typeset in Celeste 10pt
Printed and bound by Martins the Printers

# Contents

'I suppose this is where they magnetise them'

# Foreword

Mike Peyton is rightly revered in sailing circles, having graced magazines all over the world with his sketches, cartoons and stories. He's a natural story-teller with a remarkable capacity for total recall, plus an engaging and chatty conversational style.

Who else could be sharing the gripping and totally candid admission that he was an 'unsuitable son-in-law' who persuaded his girlfriend to elope and spend her honeymoon in a canoe? Her wedding presents included a sleeping bag and walking boots.

This book is all about Mike and Kathleen Peyton's ten boats. The first being that 12ft sailing canoe, *Voorlooper*, an 'impulse buy', which taught Mike the most when he knew the least and nearly caused divorce soon after he was married.

Next was *Vagrant*, a 24ft gaff-rigged centre-boarder, described as a 'penny sick' for Southend Pier day-trippers. Third was the Dutch botter, *Clementine*, a medieval-looking 40ft open boat with a large snug forepeak and a communal 12ft-wide bunk in which 'you all had to turn over together'!

*Sugar Creek*, a 30ft Colin Archer design, was the vessel that almost ship-wrecked the Peyton family, after a torn mainsail and failed engine left them at the mercy of wind and tide taking them on to the East Coast sandbank. A dramatic rescue by a North Sea ferry saw Mike passing his daughters, Hilary and Veronica, aged three and four, to safe hands as the water rose up to the bunks.

Boat number five was *Froyna,* a wooden clinker Folkboat with crouching headroom but, alas, no heater. Cruising her in winter was 'like sleeping in a snowball'. Then came *Dowsabel*, a pretty 33ft wooden yawl and *Concerto*, a fire-damaged classic wooden Vertue. Finally, Mike's trio of ferro-cement boats were launched: *Lodestone* a 40ft yawl, *Brimstone* (35ft) and *Touchstone* (38ft), the latter launched 27 years ago. All three were very basic boats. When you've spent a lifetime drawing cartoons of others' mistakes, you soon learn that back-to-basics boating is best. There's plenty of waterborne wisdom in these pages to make your sailing both safer and fun.

Paul Gelder
Editor of *Yachting Monthly* magazine

# Introduction

I consider myself lucky that in over fifty years' sailing I've always had reasonable boats, except for the first one, which taught me the most when I knew the least. My wife, when asked by the purchaser why I was selling it, replied, 'Because he wants a boat he can go to sea in.' But my boats always brought me and my crews safely home in fair weather and foul, time after time. The pleasure they gave was incalculable, something only another boat owner can appreciate.

'Do you ever think sailing's a bit overated?'

# Chapter 1
## Voorlooper

The first boat I ever bought was an impulse buy which nearly ended in my divorce, and months later, by an odd coincidence, my drowning. At that time, my wife Kath and I were living in what had been a derelict cottage. When we moved there in 1956 the cottage had no floors and no windows, but these essentials had gradually been added and we had saved enough money to have a new kitchen built to replace the lean-to shed with the sagging roof that we were currently using. We had been quoted £200 for the new kitchen and, after slowly saving up, the money was in the bank. By chance, the boat I saw for sale was also £200. As I said, it was an impulse buy. The seller, who became a good friend, kindly knocked £5 off the price when he found out it would leave us without a penny to our name.

But of course one does not make such decisions – such as spending one's all on buying a boat – lightly. I had already been introduced to sailing; almost imperceptibly I had drifted into it, and I knew already, even if only subconsciously, that it wasn't only a boat I was buying, but a way of life. I was an art student at the time of this imperceptible drifting, and if I did not actually starve in a garret I tightened my belt a few times on the floor below. I was living on a £2 a week ex-serviceman's grant, given by a grateful government

**'There's times you think more of your boat than of me'**

for helping them win the war. The grant had initially been issued on the assumption I would be living at home in Manchester where food and a bed would have been free. But I had transferred to a London art school on my own accord where my digs (bed and breakfast only) were £2 a week. I scrubbed in pubs etc to make the wherewithal to eat and I shared the digs with another ex-serviceman called Brian, a South African who had been in the Royal Navy. He was now a fireman stationed in Shoreditch and was spending some time having a look around Europe before returning home. In fact, I met him when we were both hitch-hiking in Oslo.

England in the late forties was a pretty drab, depressing place to live. It was still recovering from the years of total war: a lot of things were still rationed, shortages were the norm and many people were emigrating. After meeting in a Richmond pub, it was from one of these emigrants that Brian bought a canvas sailing canoe. As the emigrant was leaving the following day Brian had a good bargaining position, and though he bought it sight unseen it was at a price the seller couldn't refuse. The following weekend we went to the garage in Richmond where the canoe was lying and put it in the river.

The canoe was 12ft long with a 12ft mast and because of its South African antecedents it was named *Voorlooper*, which according to Brian was the Africaans name for the black boy who ran at the head of a team of oxen. The

upper reaches of the Thames by Richmond soon palled, and the most exciting times we had in that area were when we tried to milk cows from the canoe as they stood cooling themselves knee deep in river. They rarely appreciated the intrusion, hence the excitement. However, we started working our way downstream – I remember cooking breakfast one morning on the Primus in an empty lighter (our normal pull-up for the night) being overlooked by Big Ben.

It was as we travelled downstream that we learned the essentials of working our tides and of reefing early, lessons which have stood me in good stead many times since. Another thing we learnt quickly was how to patch up *Voorlooper*'s leaks. We had a ready and essential source of material in the concrete pill boxes, remnants of the war years, which dotted the sea walls in those days. The joints of these pill boxes were always sealed with tar, and it was this tar, heated in a large spoon over a fire, which we used to stick a patch of material, generally torn from a handkerchief, over the damaged area.

Obviously we had our ups and downs during our little adventures on these excursions and I do remember on one occasion being cut down to size at the end of Southend pier. I was alone on this trip for some reason and I was feeling no end of a dog singlehanding across the estuary. I was aiming for the chimneys at the mouth of the Medway, which was all I could see from my low eye level, when a voice from above floated down from the end of the pier, 'Don't spit, Alfie, you'll sink the thing.'

On another occasion Brian and I had turned in for the night on the sea wall path. The canoe and the embers of our fire were on the seaward side of the sea wall and on the other was just the blackness over featureless marshes.

We were woken up by a car driving on the rough overgrown track below us, close to where we lay in our sleeping bags. The driver turned the car around and switched off the engine and lights. It was too far from the distant road to be a courting couple, and as no one got out we were both curious about it until we dozed off again. The next vehicle to wake us was a small truck from which two men got out and started digging. As they were right under where we lay we could see they were digging up coils of copper wire, stripped and stolen from a nearby pier we found out later. The pier was part of London's air defence, having been used during the war by the Observer Corps. It was only when the digging was finished and the wire loaded that the first vehicle switched on its headlights. It was a police car, and we, unseen throughout, had had a ringside view of a very dramatic 'fair cop'.

One Christmas Eve, Brian was on duty and I was alone on *Voorlooper*. It was drizzling and I was looking for shelter. There was not a lot of it about on the Kentish marshes at that time of year, but I saw a light and, paddling towards it, found it was the anchor light of a spritsail barge. It was a powder barge loaded with ammunition for the Korean War. I tied the canoe to a lee board and climbed on board. The watchman was surprised to have a visitor but nevertheless made me welcome although unfortunately there was no way he would allow me to sleep on board: 'More than my job's worth. The boss could turn up any minute.' (And this was Christmas Eve!) However, he did tell me there was an old barn on the marshes that would suit me fine, so I paddled off into the night to look for it.

When I landed I had a welcoming committee of two curious horses – and here I made a mistake. Climbing on board the barge I hadn't pulled the spray cover over the canoe cockpit, and I now had two sodden loaves, part of my Christmas fare. As they were now useless I gave them to the horses, one each. This made them my friends for life and they accompanied me (rather too closely for comfort) as I splashed my way to the barn. It was after I had stripped off, dried myself and got into my sleeping bag that I started worrying if I had pulled the canoe far enough up to be out of the reach of the tide. Even as I vacillated I knew I would have to get up and see to it. The question now was how? Should I put my wet clothes back on or make a quick dash in my Y-fronts? I did the latter, so in writing this I have put it on record that I am one of the few men who has spent Christmas Eve running across a Kentish marsh in his Y-fronts with two horses trotting after him in close company.

4

**'According to this service-by date, only
another year and you'll have a classic liferaft'**

It was shortly after this incident that Brian asked if I would go to the Korean War with him. It was a Government scheme and the idea was that ex-servicemen could be fast-tracked there. I agreed to go with him but with one proviso. I now had a girlfriend, Kath, who I had met at the art school, and I was thinking of asking her to marry me. If she said no to my proposal I would go to Korea with Brian whenever he wanted. As it happened, Kath said yes and I had to say no to Brian – he became our best man instead. As Kath's parents didn't consider me suitable son-in-law material she had to elope, an archaic word no longer used but which meant getting married without parental consent (which one needed if under 21). My friends had a whip round to buy Kath such essential wedding presents as a sleeping bag and a decent pair of walking boots, as we were bound for the Swiss Alps, the idea being to scramble about them until my money (£40) ran out, which it did in six months.

We set off on our honeymoon in the canoe via the River Medway towards Dover, and it was on the early days of this trip that we met two well-known characters. The first was a famous barging skipper known as Tubby Blake, who with his wife as mate skippered the *Lancashire*. We had run out of water

by Aylsford lock. It was late in the day and it had just started to rain, but by chance the *Lancashire* was aground nearby. Tubby, seeing our situation, threw us a line and hauled us over the mud until we were alongside and we slept that night snug as could be in the forepeak of the *Lancashire*, on the spare sails. Years later when I read of Tubby's fame – at least among east coast cognoscenti – I basked in reflected glory.

Major General Jenkins was another character. As was our habit, whenever we had finished a trip in *Voorlooper* we tried to find someone to leave it with so that they could use it until we returned. Scout troops were the ideal crowd for this, so we arrived at the troop affiliated to Tonbridge school. It was run by Major General Jenkins. If, as he told us kindly, we found his rank too much of a mouthful, we could call him 'Blue Eagle'! It was years later in Dover harbour, when tied alongside a tug called *Major General Jenkins,* that I discovered from the skipper of the tug and all his crew of Rover Scouts what a paragon the Major General had been.

These incidents reflect the fact that although I had done no serious sailing as such, I had done enough messing about on the water to be able to visualise the vast potential of my £200 impulse buy: the odd things that happened, the type of people one met. Later Kath was to say, proudly I like to think, that she had the only gaff-rigged kitchen in Essex. But not at the time. In fact she later told me she was so incensed she didn't speak to me for a week. And what really annoyed her was that I was so taken up with the new purchase I didn't even notice.

# Chapter 2
## Vagrant

The boat I had bought was a 24ft x 8ft x 1.6ft gaff-rigged centreboarder. Originally a cutter, *Vagrant* was now a sloop, having had her bowsprit removed – to her detriment as I found out later. She had worked for her living taking holidaymakers out to the end of Southend Pier and back, a penny sick, as they were known. She had no side decks. Whoever had bought her from this trade had built up her topsides by about two feet and decked them over right up to the stem head. When you climbed out of the cockpit you had to be quick on your feet, for in those days guardrails and pulpits were unheard of.

As I made my maiden voyage in *Vagrant*, other momentous happenings were going on in the world, one being the Hungarian Revolution. An upshot of this is that I had a Hungarian crew member on board. Many Hungarians had had to flee their country and the nation as a whole had been asked to take them in. We got Gabor. The other crew member was Tommy. He and I had served together in the Eighth Army in North Africa and as Churchill wrote: need one say more?

The boat had an engine, a 10hp Brooke, but it wasn't running as our current book of instruction, a Penguin paperback called *Sailing* by Peter

Heaton (one of the finest books in English literature I might add), advised us to eschew using the engine until we could handle the yacht under sail. I am very good at eschewing and I foolishly eschewed.

I doubt if any yacht went to sea with such a crew of tyros. In fact we didn't actually intend to go to sea. We left the creek at high water, carried the tide down the Crouch with a fair wind in a state of bliss until we arrived at Shore Ends. Here, when we wanted to come back, we couldn't. The change from cutter to sloop and the removal of her bowsprit and jib had unbalanced *Vagrant* far beyond our experience to correct. We hadn't the gumption to think to anchor and wait for the tide to change. Peter Heaton had long since disintegrated in the bilge water so we did the only thing we knew how and continued running before the wind.

For many years I saved a newspaper cutting of which I was inordinately proud because it told how on that day, because of strong winds, racing was cancelled in the River Blackwater. And on that day we bucketed across the Blackwater towards Mersea willy nilly. We had an extra scare when Gabor frantically flipped through his new English–Hungarian dictionary and,

pointing into the cabin, shouted, 'Puddle! Puddle!' This was an understatement as the cabin sole was awash. The reason was that every time *Vagrant* pounded the centreboard case, it grew two watery ears where the centre-board bolt was. As a maiden voyage it was memorable and it was the first step in the start of a way of life.

**Vagrant, my first £200 boat.**

Along with half a dozen other small boats, *Vagrant* was kept in a mud berth in Clements Green Creek off the River Crouch. Clements Green is a tidal creek and was only a short walk over the fields from our cottage. The cottage we now lived in had been built on what had been known as Plot Land, given that name because early speculators had brought East Enders down to the area hoping to sell them a one acre plot.

The end result was that the area (South Woodham Ferrers) became a criss cross of dirt roads that connected these plots, which now contained shacks, sheds, old railway carriages, caravans, bungalows, and the odd brick-built cottage such as ours. By great good fortune we were on the outskirts of these plots, although it was undoubtedly reclaimed marsh and, because the cottage was below sea level, we paid sea drainage rates.

The creek became the nucleus of our life, and into this milieu – the creek, the boats, their impecunious but enthusiastic owners and their doings – we fitted in as an oar in a rowlock. The mainspring of Clements Green was Peter Pointer, who lived by the creek. A glider pilot during the war, he had subsequently sailed in square rig and now built plywood dinghies in a shed just behind the sea wall. All his profit must have gone on bird food as morning and evening he fed hundreds of wild birds. He was like St Francis as he stood there strewing the feed. At one time I thought Clements Green and its denizens were unique, but later I realised every tidal creek attracted approximately the same type of character. Fenn Creek (the next creek west) had an architect who had built himself a wooden house like a black ridge tent. Featureless on three sides, it was all glass where it faced the creek. It was close enough that at high water he could dive in from his living-room window. Also in Fenn Creek was an old sea captain, Captain Coward, who at high springs had to sit on a chair on his table along with a supply of dry firewood, waiting for the ebb because his floor was awash.

But it was Clements Green that was our creek. From this base we pottered about the east coast, invariably with our distinguishing flag hoist of drying nappies, for we now had two daughters. There were generally about six or seven boats in the creek, mostly in mud berths, and as I came over the sea wall I only had to look for which chimney was smoking (they all had stoves) or which hatch was open to know where I would have my first cup of tea of the day. Both boats and owners were a mixed bag. There was a home-built barge yacht, literally a 24ft box with a pointed end. Even the owner admitted her performance was poor and told the story of racing a mattress down the River Crouch – unfortunately it beat him because it got a better slant in Cliff Reach.

There was a smack CK 21 renamed *Maria* that the owner Tom Bolton had bought for £10, and recouped the cost by selling the eels he caught in the bilges. Both Kath and I have vivid memories of our first sight of Tom. He was sailing into the creek in his previous boat, a steel lifeboat conversion called

**'It's in the bag, boys – kite down – genny in – gybe ove...'**

*Pla-ta*. Tom worked for the PLA (the Port of London Authority). He had his regular crew on board: his young daughter and his dog, a black mongrel. Coming in to anchor, he was swinging a grapnel which was actually an iron bar with about ten hooks attached, normally used for dragging lock basins when there was a search for a body.

For a time there was an 18ft double ender called *Snipe*, which was later to come to a tragic end. Then there was a small ex-Broads boat with minimum freeboard. Her owner Frank was a journalist and an ex naval signaller – although in those days yachtsmen were expected to know some basic Morse, his speed in sending it surprised a few harbour officials.

Looking back on those halcyon days I realise the truth in the saying that you learn more from your first boat than from any that follow. To pay for this way of life Kath wrote and, what was more to the point, sold what was termed 'the teenage novel'. On my part I illustrated magazines, one of which, *The New Scientist*, I was to work for, one day a week, for over thirty years. In fact for one year, when I wanted the money for a bigger boat, I worked full time as the Art Editor as well as keeping up with my freelance work. I got very friendly with one of the journalists who was developing an exposure suit for pilots who had to bale out over the sea. So *Vagrant* started justifying her existence, often sailing on sea trials for the suit.

Another source of income was a regular cartoon, which I drew for the magazine *Commercial Motor*. As my only knowledge of commercial vehicles was what I had found out when hitching home as a student and reading back numbers of the magazine, it seemed logical that I could do the same for the yachting press. But this was not to be. In those days yachting was a serious business. Ensigns were hoisted at daybreak and were struck at sunset – on the minute, I might add. In proper yachting circles standards were upheld. The denizens of Clements Green Creek, however enthusiastic, did not have them. In fact, they were the first 'yotties' just emerging, as from primeval

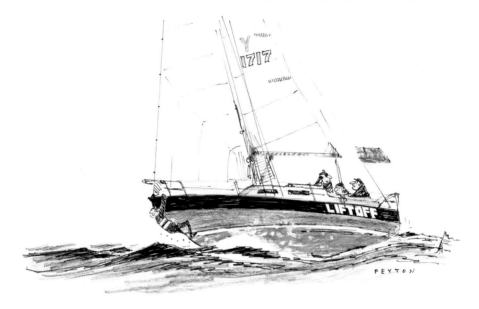

'I could have sworn I saw a windsurfer'

mud. My rejection slips from yachting magazines for the sailing cartoons which I'd submitted to them could have papered a room.

Though much is now forgotten, Kath and I both remember our first anchorage in Pyefleet Creek. We were the only yacht in the creek, sharing it with seven motormen who were also sheltering there. Motorman was the name given to spritsail barges that had shipped their topmasts and bowsprits and had a motor installed. Though we did not realise it then we were seeing the end of an era. The only two barges still operating under sail, which we

used to see underway, were the *Cambria* and the *Anglia*. It was probably symbolic that the last time I saw the *Anglia* she was in a flat calm in the Swin and was taking a line from a motorman. Later I saw the skipper of the *Cambria*, Bob Roberts, who was known throughout the length and breadth of the east coast and in the back bar of The Plough and Sail in Paglesham. The walls of the bar were then almost completely covered with sepia prints of all the barges, bawleys and smacks that had been launched from Shuttlewoods shed; a gallery of local maritime history. Bob was a living part of this history and he was doing what he was famous for that night: singing the old seamen's songs of the east coast, 'Stormy Old Weather', 'A is for the Anchor', etc. He was belting them out to an appreciative audience of yachtsmen and villagers, who had probably built the boats whose sepia prints adorned the walls. It was then that an attractive girl in a mini skirt made a request... I was near enough to hear what it was: it was from another world, a song of Nancy Sinatra's, 'These Boots are Made for Walking'. The jukebox was close behind.

The riding light says it all.
Vagrant has dragged her anchor.

Our learning experience with *Vagrant* continued, and one day we went aground in the Colne opposite Alresford Creek. In my ignorance I was cutting out the sweep of the buoyed channel of High Park Corner and though I was annoyed when *Vagrant* grounded, it turned out for the best. It was fool's luck. That same night a small yacht, also anchored in the Colne, was hit by one of the many coasters that used the Colne at high water on their way up to Colchester. The two men on board were drowned. The tinny little riding light that many impecunious yachtsmen of the time used, me included, was replaced on *Vagrant* by a Tilley lamp. But the more I sailed *Vagrant* and the more she taught me, the more I realised that she was no longer the boat for me. I had grown out of her.

# Chapter 3

## Clementine

We sold *Vagrant* to a banana importer from Birmingham. I remember this because he brought me a hand of green bananas when he came to take *Vagrant* away. I also remember Kath's candid reply to his query, 'Why is Mike selling *Vagrant*?' 'Because he wants a boat he can go to sea in' was her instant reply. I was appalled, but it was true and it made no difference to the sale. The banana importer did not want to go to sea. *Vagrant* was now destined to spend her days as a floating caravan on the Grand Union Canal. To further this end I delivered her to London and saw her into the Canal.

By now a keen yachtsman (my wife said besotted), it was obvious I had to get another boat, and I already knew what it was and where it was coming from. The local pub in South Woodham was losing its attraction because nobody talked about boats, whereas The Ferry Boat in Fambridge, where they did, became my local. It was a conversation I had overheard there that decided me. A yachtsman had just come back from a cruise in Holland, and he mentioned that because of the polderisation of the Isselmeer (or the Zuider Zee as it was then known), the fishing harbours surrounding it would soon be landlocked and the fishing boats would be useless. They were all for sale and it was a buyer's market. Shortly after hearing this conversation I was on the ferry to Holland, complete with a chart of the North Sea and a hand bearing compass just in case. Fortunately the friend I went with had a Dutch connection – Dirk. Dirk had been in the Royal Navy, he spoke English and had a car, and together we saw dozens of botters in a variety of harbours. They were all tarred black except one, *EB 49* in Elburg, which was varnished. That was the one I bought, my reasoning being that only someone proud of his boat in all respects would varnish it. I ignored the fact that the wooden clogged, baggy-trousered fisherman, to whom I paid £400 for it, had two hulking sons to help maintain his botter in that condition. He even gave me his recipe for mixing the varnish.

Two weeks later, three of us went over to Holland to bring *EB 49* back. John had an amazing amount of sea time, but as it was during the war as a midshipman on an aircraft carrier, this experience was discounted. Then there was Gordon, also ex Navy, whose way of life and experience made him the natural skipper. He worked throughout the winter scrimping and saving and in spring he bought a boat (there were always plenty of small wooden boats for sale, some of whose owners had not come back from the war) and sailed away for the summer. Returning to the UK at the end of summer he sold the boat, advertising it truthfully as 'Cruised extensively', and repeated the procedure.

'I bet that's ruined somebody's weekend'

For some reason I no longer remember, but it was probably excitement, we left Elburg in *EB 49* without my provisioning her. We existed on boiled sweets and cold water until we reached an industrial backwater in Amsterdam, by which time we were famished. We clambered over the gates of the yard whose quay we had tied up in with one thought in our minds: FOOD. We had a stroke of luck in getting a taxi in the lonely dockland road we dropped into. In those days not every Dutchman spoke English and whether in our sign language we rubbed too low, or the taxi man jumped to his own conclusions, but he delivered us to a brothel. The Madam took the loss of trade in good spirit when the mistake was pointed out, and directed our driver to take us to a restaurant with a proviso, which we fortunately had bethought of, that he had to pick us up there later and deliver us to where he had picked us up from as only he knew where *EB 49* was lying.

Most people can remember some exceptional meal they have enjoyed in a lifetime, the best meal they have ever eaten. That was a good one, but the *best ever* happened on the way home, and only a yachtsman can truly appreciate it. We left Ijmuiden late November and as we wallowed out into the grey North Sea I was sick, sick as a dog, and stayed that way until there wasn't a retch left in me. All that time Gordon and John stood my watch until I realised I was over the worst. I staggered out to where Gordon was at the helm and took the tiller. Before he disappeared to his bunk he asked if I wanted anything. My reply was 'Food'. After ensuring it wasn't dry bread I required, he left me. When he reappeared he was carrying the frying pan containing what could only be described as a full English – plus. On a foundation of fried bread there was well done bacon, sausages, eggs, beans and tomatoes and a large spoon. I pegged the tiller, which you can do on a botter, and set to. While I was so engaged, Gordon reappeared. At my feet was a large gimballed compass contained in a box about 2ft x 2ft. He balanced a mug of tea on the centre of the gimballed compass and I was alone. As I was eating this magnificent meal, appreciated as only a famished man can appreciate food, I realised I must be, at that moment in time, one of the luckiest men in the world. There I was, master before God of a stout craft that could sail the seven seas with a trusty crew below. Above, the tanned sails were straining and the long red bob at the masthead was stiff before a fair north-easterly. She breasted the waves like a gull...or did I say wallowing?

We had an uneventful sail home except for one small incident. Navigation

in those pre-GPS days was a bit of an art and you needed all the help you could get. In our case we needed time. We could not agree whether we were on British or Continental time. It obviously made a difference to the tidal sets shown on the tidal diamonds on the chart so we decided to ask someone. It must have been the Shipwash light vessel that was convenient and we ran down towards it. Our lights had obviously been seen because we saw a figure silhouetted against the

**Clementine bought for £400 in Holland when the Zuider Zee was reclaimed from the sea.**

inside light as he opened a door to come on deck. We were close enough to shout to him 'What time is it?' He gave us the answer and then asked 'What ship is that?' and all I could reply was 'I don't know' before we sluiced past into the darkness. He must have thought we were idiots.

Finding a name for the botter had initially seemed straightforward as we had handed over the money for her on November the fifth, but Guy Fawkes did not appeal, so we thought of the sail number and Fortyniner. This was on the right track, as the song puts it: 'a miner Fortyniner and his daughter Clementine'. So *Clementine* she became and we ignored the bit about 'sank beneath the foaming brine'.

*Clementine* fitted into the east coast (at least in the way we sailed) to the manner born, but she had one great drawback – she was labour intensive. For a man whose family crew consisted of Kath (eight stone) and Hilary and Veronica (three and two years old) she was hard work. Even my male crews had a saying that three trips on *Clementine* entitled you to a Botter Campaign medal. Metaphorically speaking, some had rows of medals, yet they came back for more. Though an open boat, she had a large snug forepeak forward of the mast, and in this forepeak there was a coal-heated oven cum stove. She also had a communal bunk 12ft wide. Generally you had ample room but there were times you all had to turn over together.

Medieval in appearance as *Clementine* was, she had many advanced features. Her only rigging was her forestay which was an iron bar, decades before rod rigging. The lee boards had airfoil sections. The characteristic short gaff was the predecessor of many hotshot boats of the present day and the fish well was a brilliant bit of lateral thinking. She also had a 13hp Kromhaut diesel but that never worked for many weeks. Another bit of lateral thinking was that you baled her out with a wooden shovel. This shovel had high sides that fitted almost exactly between two of her substantial frames, and if you were quick enough (in fact you had to be) you could shovel a fair amount of water into the fish well.

Even her retractable bowsprit has been rediscovered, though *Clementine*'s was about the same size as a telegraph pole and took three men standing astride it to ship it without too much strain. Her comprehensive collection of quants were designed by some long-gone Dutchmen. They all had different ends for the bottom you were pushing off from and they were efficient. One quant was designed as a booming out pole for a sail they set aft and I was pleased I had been curious enough to ask Dirk why all the topping lifts on the botters we had looked at were in two lengths and knotted together, about two foot from the boom end, rather than in one length of rope. He found out that the length that came from the masthead was the hoist they used when they boomed out a sail aft. Years later I was able to explain this fact, with pleasure I admit, to a curious curator in the boat model section of the Science

**Hilary and Veronica, a light-weight crew for a heavyweight boat.**

Museum. He had noticed the knot in the topping lifts of all the models they had but did not know the purpose of them.

The break in the topping lift may have had another use; one which I would like to believe. One of my regular crew gave me a book which had been translated from the Dutch, called *The Lost Sea*. It was a story based on the lives of the early fishermen of the Zuider Zee, they had fishing in

common but were divided by religion. They were either Catholic or Calvanist and if they met at sea they fought. The battles could be between the fishing fleets of the various harbour or individual craft but either way the end result was the same. The victors debagged the losers and sailed away with the losers' baggy trousers flying from their masthead. Fact or fiction or fifty/fifty, it would give another use for the knot in the topping lift of a botter – hauling up baggy trousers.

I'd learned more from *Vagrant* in what is termed 'the hard way' than in any of the boats that followed her. But on *Clementine* I was often sailing with other yachtsmen, most of whom had far more experience than me. Gordon is a good example. I learnt from them and they influenced me a lot. But why didn't they sail botters when there were plenty available and going cheap? As I got more experience I realised a 40ft open boat with heavy gear was no longer the boat for me and so *Clementine* was put up for sale.

The sale triggered an odd experience and I assure you it is true in all respects. I had sold *Clementine* and the new owner was coming to collect her that afternoon from the creek, when the tide served. She was bound for the upper reaches of the Thames to be converted into a house boat. The day prior to this I went on board and found her leaking through two jets of water just opposite the mast. It had been a dry summer and some caulking had fallen out. When the tide left her I hammered some new lengths of caulking in. When the new owner arrived the next day, we were having a coffee at our cottage and he told us he had been at a drinks party in South Kensington the evening before. He had told a man at the party that he had just bought a boat and the reply he got was, 'Yes, I can see it now. As you look at it from the front it is very big and brown,' which is a perfect description of a varnished botter with its swept-up bow. He then continued, 'and as you look at it from the front on the right hand side there are two jets of water coming in'. I choked on my coffee then told him all. Seemingly the man he had been speaking to had a psychic gift and was often called in by the police, but was very hit and miss in what he could tell them. But he had been spot on the target this time.

# Chapter 4

## Sugar Creek

By now, being an avid reader of yachting magazines, having read almost every sailing book the local library could offer, and having more experienced sailing friends, I was far more selective in what I wanted from a boat. The one I bought next was of impeccable antecedents in that day and age. She was a heavily built 30ft gaff cutter rigged Colin Archer with 10.6ft beam, a 4.6ft draught and fitted with a 7hp Sleipner petrol paraffin engine. She had a very small cockpit about 2ft x 2ft and you went down to your armpits, so I put in a removable false bottom to make it waist deep. At that time a Colin Archer was considered the sea boat par excellence. I bought her from a Frenchman who was living in England and he had bought her from an American Mormon, hence her name *Sugar Creek* – Sugar Creek being the site of some Mormon skirmish.

The attraction was that I could handle her alone. In those pre-marina days harbours were free and looked on as places of refuge and *Sugar* was often left in various harbours, her heavy construction allowing her to hold her own with the help of a few scooter tyres. Obviously a boat like this had to be used and after a few shakedown trips locally, a long haul was planned, with the destination of San Sebastian in Spain.

**Sugar Creek, a small Colin Archer.**

The crew were John who had crewed back from Holland on *Clementine*; Riq, a friend of his who measured isotopes at CERN for a living; and Jack who, like me, worked as a free-lance commercial artist. I chose San Sebastian for our destination because I was hedging my bets. Though I was going to evening classes on navigation at least twice a week, I reasoned that once we had rounded Ushant and saw land lying north and south we should steer south and if it was lying east and west we should go east. Either way San Sebastian would appear, and so it proved.

However, we did get some help from two Spanish fishing boats, who made a detour to come close, and with their registration of BB we assumed they were from Bilbao. When they left us, Riq, who was a devout Catholic, said 'They will probably be going home for the feast of Corpus Christi.' The penny dropped: they were not changing one area of the Bay for another; they were heading for Bilbao. We took a bearing on their course, transferred it to the chart starting from Bilbao and it crossed our course line only a whisker from our estimated position. It was simply an extension of barking dog navigation.

We had a friendly welcome to San Sebastian. English yachts were not common then, and as the war had only been over about seven years, people were well disposed to the British. In the first bar we went into, four drinks were put before us, on the house. We were in there again later when it seemed the harbour suddenly went mad. Fishermen were scrambling on board their boats, starting up engines; even small boats were being rowed out. In minutes the harbour was empty except for us. We found out later that

**'That's the beacon alright, it always has cormorants on it'**

a huge shoal of sardines had been sighted in the vicinity, and for days afterwards the town reeked of frying sardines as the vendors hawked their wares.

In San Sebastian we had a memorable dining disappointment. On the day we arrived we went into a restaurant to celebrate the longest passage any of us had made under sail. We got it across to the waiter that we wanted the best meal the house could offer. It was obvious he'd got the message and we sat back in pleasant anticipation. When it arrived it looked like pieces of sago pudding in whitewash. Our long-awaited meal turned into a disaster, not only because we were disappointed but because it seemed the entire restaurant and staff were disappointed at our disappointment. I read later that the speciality of the house, indeed the area, was the edible matter found in the head of a hake: its brain. I was the only one of the four who felt duty bound to eat it.

On the return trip we called in at La Rochelle, where the huge slabs of concrete that had covered the German U Boat pens were still lying higgledy piggledy from their last British air raid. It was where the classic German film

*Das Boot* ended. Also in the harbour was an area where the deep, beamy hulks of old tunny fishing boats were rotting away like the cadavers in an elephants' graveyard. We came up the Channel in three tacks and off Boulogne we had a reminder of a change in the way of the sea. Three French corvettes were steaming up the channel ahead in line and I dipped my ensign to the leader. An easy matter as all I had to do was reach aft. The reply was instant: a door in the bridge house opened and a matelot, pulling his oilskin coat on, for it was raining, scurried aft and did the honours. I dipped to the second corvette and the procedure was repeated but when I dipped my ensign to the third corvette a window slid open in the side of the bridge house, a rigid arm appeared and I received an emphatic, stiff, two-fingered salute.

One Easter trip to Ostende was unforgettable. Easter was the beginning of the sailing season as far as the crew was concerned – a long weekend, and it was invariably Ostende. As it is an 80 mile passage a night sail is obvious and that particular night was magical. There was a moon you could read the chart by, we had a topsail breeze and all that that entails, a good wind, and a fair wind. At times I stood in the bows and looked up at the sails almost ethereal in the moonlight. The shadows from the shrouds and rigging backed and filled across the canvas as the boat dipped and swayed across the smooth water.

Looking aft I could see my companions by the cockpit and hear the murmur of their voices, the occasional laugh, the glow of a cigarette, and sometimes a spark from the chimney as it flew away towards the stars. It was a magical night and we all knew it. It was a rare moment in time when it seemed as if so much had combined to give us a heightened sense of pleasure and all we had to do was to be there and appreciate it. Which we did, throughout the night. We did nothing else; so when dawn appeared ahead 'and put the stars to flight' none of us had had any sleep and we were tired and crotchety, but we had had our moment.

The return trip was different, the forecast was not the best but the workaday world called and off we set. We were off the North Hinder when we found that because of an oversight, both Primuses were out of paraffin and we were unable to make the essential cups of tea. To make the filling of the Primus an easier job I decided to heave to. A few minutes' job in harbour now became a major operation.

Someone braced to in a bunk and held a Primus and funnel while the one with the paraffin seized his moment. The Primus filled, it was easy to

**'Humber, Thames, Dover, gale eight, severe gale nine,
occasionally storm force ten'**

persuade ourselves that we would enjoy our cuppa more with the relative comfort from *Sugar*'s best point of sailing – hove to. With the tea drunk, night falling and the wind getting up, we put our last reef in, tied a Tilley to the boom gallows and turned in. It was only when we got back to the Crouch that we heard that another local boat, *Alley Sloper* (which had left Ostende with us), had lost a man overboard. He had been coming on watch, actually on the bridge deck, when a wave came on board and swept him away into the darkness, still warm from his sleeping bag, to a cold, lonely and horrific death.

*Sugar Creek* served us well, especially when she had a free wind, and we actually raced her in the first Old Gaffers Race in 1962 in which we came a lonely fifth, finishing at 01:30. I've always been pleased that I insisted we rounded the last mark in a light wind and against a foul tide, against the wishes of my fed up crew. 'Start the engine, no one will ever know' was their advice. Now all these years later I can say in all honesty we were fifth in the first Old Gaffers Race. On that race we had been asked if we could take a professional photographer on board, which I did, and he was the most vociferous in wanting me to start the engine. This was understandable, as he had

23

expected to be put ashore in Harwich in the late afternoon – not the small hours of the morning. Nevertheless, he did me a good turn. I assumed his camera was a German Rolliflex, which at that time cost two or three hundred pounds, but he told me it was a Japanese copy – a Yashikamat that cost £40. So I bought one and started selling photos to the yachting press. I have no doubt that my art training helped but I was getting a lot of sailing in and the camera was always hanging ready, just inside the doghouse. One year I supplied 25 per cent of the covers used by the yachting magazines.

The year after the first Old Gaffers Race, *Sugar Creek* was involved in a disaster. John, who had sailed both from Holland and to San Sebastian with me, bought a boat of his own. It was one that Gordon had once owned – *Snipe,* an 18ft gaff-rigged double ender. She was well known in her day as one of the boats owned by a prominent east coast writer, Francis B Cooke, who started one of his books, '*Snipe* was launched on the day of Queen Victoria's Jubilee'.

*Snipe* was lying in Ramsgate and five of us – Kath, Tom Bolton, two brothers – named Young – and myself, sailed over to accompany them to the Crouch. We found them fitting a mast. John had bought her without one and he, together with a friend Jack Worsley, had simply gone to the nearest hop field and brought back a suitable hop pole. Both Tom and the Young brothers wanted to sail back on *Snipe* along with John and Jack, and to decide the matter they cut cards for the privilege. Fate had it that Tom won. We towed them out of Ramsgate at about midnight, then cast them off. We then had

**Snipe from Clementine**

the last of the ebb to get to the North Foreland in time to catch the first of the flood into the Thames and rendezvous off Whitstable. This was an acknowledged method for engine-less boats to use the tides to cross the Thames Estuary: in along the Kentish shore on the flood and out via the Swin on the ebb.

We crossed tacks with them once after we rounded the Foreland and we never saw them

again. The wreckage of *Snipe* was found and Jack's body, nothing else. John and Tom were never found. It seemed ironic that they survived the war – John as a midshipman on an aircraft carrier, Tom going through Europe as a sapper in the Engineers, and Jack as an infantry sergeant in Burma – to die as they did, doing what they enjoyed most.

When Kath went to tell Tom's wife that he had drowned she was greeted as she opened the door, 'Is that you, Tom? Thank heavens you're back. That dog of yours started whimpering and whining at two in the morning and it's never stopped since.' The dog was inconsolable and so badly affected that it had to be put down. A black mongrel about fifty miles away from the scene was the first to know of the tragedy.

We attended the inquest, where it was assumed that they had gone onto the Margate Sands and *Snipe* had broken up, but later I came to a different conclusion. They were too experienced to go on the sands, as they had the shore lights to tell them if they had been too far out, and even if they had gone on the sands, with *Snipe* having only a 3ft draught they would have gone over the side and pushed her off. It was the wreckage of *Snipe* that made me think otherwise. The wreckage found was exactly half a boat: one complete side of the hull. *Snipe* was over seventy years old and relatively lightly built. I remembered that when we had joined them in Ramsgate they had been rigging the mast, and they didn't have bottle screws so they used cord. It went from the eyes in the shrouds and led through the eyes in the chain plates a number of times. It was a natural fibre cord and I now realised that when it got wet it would shrink. It was simply a physical law, and the cord was well able to exert the pressure to force the mast onto the keel and split the boat in two and none of us had thought of it.

Though we missed the liveliness of Tom, it was John and Jack, with whom we had sailed a lot, that we best remember. In one aspect this was because of music. They were both classical music buffs and when conditions were fair they would sprawl in the cockpit and go through some favourite symphony. They would take all the parts between themselves, in what the Irish term 'mouth music'. John, in the modulated tones befitting a Winchester man, and Jack with his deep West Country accent that you could cut with a knife. Tom himself is remembered annually in the East Coast Old Gaffers race for the Tom Bolton cup. It was intended to be in memory of the three of them but Tom had entered his smack in the first race, whereas John and Jack had only crewed.

It was when I owned *Sugar Creek* that I sold my first yachting cartoon. It was a satisfying week for me when, after sending innumerable cartoon ideas to all the yachting magazines, three editors, two of monthly magazines and one of a new fortnightly, *Yachting and Boating*, wrote to me in the same week asking if I would call and see them.

I went to the fortnightly magazine, now defunct, as at that time I could have kept a daily magazine supplied with yachting cartoons. The editor, Charlie Jones, I now worked for knew nothing about sailing, just editing, so to get experience of sailing he sailed with me and we became good friends. During the war he had been in the retreat from France and a remark he made still brings him to mind. One weekend we sailed to Calais and as we entered the harbour he pointed to the lighthouse and said, 'The last time I saw that I was on top of it with a Bren gun.'

Charlie lost his job on a matter of principle. In 1968-9 the *Sunday Times* sponsored a Singlehanded Around the World Race, with a prize of £5,000. The race is now remembered for the winner Robin Knox-Johnston and the apparent suicide of Donald Crowhurst. Charlie wrote an editorial on the fact that commercial pressures were now coming into the sailing scene. Now, with

'Typical of your mother, the first day of Cowes week'

hindsight, he was right, but the magazine was sued, lost the case and Charlie lost his job. Knox-Johnston gave his prize money to Crowhurst's widow.

One of the other editors who had asked me to visit him was Bernard Hayman, of *Yachting World*. In our meeting he pointed out that a detail in one cartoon – the siting of a winch – was incorrect, and this made me realise that I could not work for such a pedant, especially as I had not got any winches on my boat but plenty of artist's licence. Bernard and I subsequently became quite friendly and he told me he always regretted not giving me a job. My cartoons started appearing regularly in *Yachts and Yachting*, which I soon found out had a serious risk attached. The editor, Peter Cooke, lived about six miles from me and often I delivered the cartoons by hand. Peter brewed his own beer and invariably I was asked to give my opinion of his latest batch. The alcoholic content was up to him, and in those days before breathalysers I remember many an evening leaving his house and having enough sense to put the car in second or third gear until I reached home.

Owning *Sugar Creek* altered our way of sailing. One reason was that we became 'proper yachtsmen', as we left the creek and moved *Sugar*, as we abbreviated her name, to swinging moorings at Fambridge. We paid mooring fees and three miles downriver we came into contact with proper yachtsmen. There were about thirty moorings there at that time, mostly with sound wooden cruising boats on them. They were about fifty/fifty gaff and bermudian and few were over 30ft. The owners, though friendly, we never became familiar with. Some of the yachtsmen at Fambridge put white covers to their yachting caps on the day that the Navy decided it was summer time. Their ensigns were hoisted at daybreak and struck at sunset, often to the minute.

But the main alteration was because we came in contact with Old Mick and Mrs Mick. Old Mick was the name given to the Mr Meiklejohn who ran the moorings and Mrs Mick was his wife and kept the books. It was a very exclusive mooring as Old Mick was very choosy as to who he accepted, and unless you came up to his standards and he liked your boat you had little chance of getting a mooring there. Though there was no club, there was a clique which was at least comparable. There was also the equivalent of a clubhouse – 'The Shed' – which stood on the sea wall and had started life as a prefabricated hospital in the Crimean War. People used to gather on a Sunday evening as they returned from their weekend's sail and watch the latecomers pick up their moorings, always under sail.

In the shed, which was actually Old Mick's workshop, was a large pot-bellied stove. From this stove Mrs Mick dispensed the tea, and I can assure you that you had to be there some time before you were asked if you would like a cup of tea. The shed emptied according to the train times to London, as few people drove down, and Fambridge station was a good mile away. At the start of the weekend, supplies, ordered midweek by postcard, would be left outside the village shop in a cardboard box with the boat's name written on it. With hindsight I now realise that the yachtsmen who kept their boats at Fambridge were divided by the then prevalent class system, and Old Mick, once so particular as to who he accepted on the Fambridge moorings, was thinking of retirement and realised the more moorings he had occupied the better.

'What's kept you? I've been waiting hours to pick you up!'

As I got to know Old Mick and as he found out about my way of life, with its variable hours, he started asking me and a couple of others to do boat deliveries – boats that had been bought on some other moorings and needed to come to Fambridge, or boats that had been sold at Fambridge and needed to go elsewhere. These trips were invariably unpaid, sometimes not even expenses, as generally they were relatively local and we did it for the interest

of sailing on another boat. These trips, which always started on a Friday night, could be summed up in two ways. One was as your torch, or flashlight as they were then known, traversed the boat, if the only shiny reflection was from the pump handle – that told you a lot. The other extreme was if the boat had hemp halyards, an expensive luxury in those days.

These delivery trips were generally between the east coast and the Solent. One of them had tragic consequences. I was asked to deliver a 30ft gaffer to Yarmouth on the Isle of Wight and asked a friend John if he fancied coming along as crew. As always, he agreed. He was also a freelance artist, an animator who lived locally and wasn't tied down by normal office hours. The boat had just had a new engine installed and it was on the way down the River Crouch to Burnham when the throttle lever broke off due to a flaw in the metal. As the engine had been installed by an engineering firm in Burnham we left it in their hands and returned home for the night. For John it seemed a lucky break in all respects, as his wife told him someone had just rung up, offering him two months' work in Canada. The unexpected break allowed him to go up to London, meet his prospective employer and return in time to catch the following day's tide. On the trip down the Channel John referred to the throttle lever as his lucky charm. The delivery trip finished, John disappeared for Canada, and while he was there he seized on the opportunity to go white water rafting. The raft he was on overturned and John was drowned.

I did quite a few delivery trips, because professional delivery skippers were only just appearing on the scene. But it was a trip to bring a new boat back from Gdansk in Poland that made a big impact in Fambridge. The trip itself was uneventful except for its insight into life behind the Iron Curtain, and the fact that the keel fell off the boat two days after we returned which could have been fatal for the five crew if it had happened during the North Sea crossing. However, the boat, a 33ft Kings Amethyst, was replaced, and to all intents and purposes it became the yacht of one of the delivery crew, Jimmy Green. Jimmy maintained it for the owner, who barely used it, and sailed it for himself.

Jimmy was ex-Navy, but didn't put a white top to his yachting cap when summer commenced as he didn't have a yachting cap. He had tried living in New Zealand after the war but returned because, as he told me, all they talked about was sheep and rugby. Jimmy lived in the village and he was a

'Never mind what Adlard and Erroll did,
what's Jimmy Green going to do?'

big gregarious friendly character who liked his beer, sailing and parties – probably in that order.

The yacht, *Tarika*, became the flagship of the Flexible Yacht Club. The members were a collection of individuals who mostly had just discovered yachting and were doing it in their self-built boats. Marine ply was the flavour of the month and there was a Lightcrest built by Ian Griffiths, the headmaster of a local school, an Eventide built by Mick the Brick, obviously a bricklayer, and two Buccaneers. All were engineless. They were flexible because they preferred a fair wind to beating. Many plans discussed in the Ferry Boat Inn on a Sunday evening were discarded the following weekend to take the opportunity of using a fair wind. We also had a burgee which could be had for the asking in any garage in Ostende. It was for Heineken beer and was considered appropriate. Another club member also had a boat that came into her own in winter when she was in her mudberth. This was *Gladys*, a 40ft bawley, with a large comfortable cabin. She also had a brass plaque screwed to her main beam confirming she had taken troops off the beaches at Dunkirk.

One of the crew who had been on the trip to bring *Tarika* back from Poland was Reg Watson. He lived in Fambridge in the house nearest the Ferry Boat Inn and had been the ferry man when the ferry had been in operation. He had also been a Thames barge skipper in the 1914–18 war and used to spin yarns about those times. Reg was also involved in Hitler's war as the cox'n of an Air Sea Rescue boat. His job was to pick up pilots who had had to bail out over the estuary. He told me that if the East End, where he came from, had had a rough night from the Luftwaffe the night before, he never picked up any Germans.

Reg's stories gave Kath the idea of writing about the barges and their crew and to get the background reference she needed we sailed over to Calais and stayed there, living on the boat. The only drawback with living on board in the harbour was the fact that every day at high water the sewage of the town was discharged into it. They relied on the ebb to remove it.

To keep my one day a week job going at the *New Scientist* magazine I was able to take a daily return flight from Calais to Southend for £5 and after I had sold the duty free, which I bought on the plane, in the *New Scientist* office I was in pocket.

We often sailed in company for a specific reason. They were what we referred to as duty free runs, which meant sailing abroad to get the drink for the next party. Some of the wives or partners of the skippers were willing crew on these runs but some were press-ganged into it. They would be taken on board, made comfortable in their bunks and given a couple of sleeping tablets. They were there solely to be able to claim their duty free quota, and Jimmy's easy-going wife Ann slept through many a Channel crossing.

One party resulting from one of these duty free trips was in fancy dress, and as it coincided with a high tide I still remember it. The high tide was necessary to get *Thyatira*, the Lightcrest, into a floating dry dock that had been adapted out of a wooden swim-headed lighter called the *Lillian*. The lighter, whose bows had been cut off almost to water level, was moored parallel to the sea wall in Clements Green creek and sat on the saltings at low water. Come high water, *Thyatira* was floated in and as the tide left her she would be shored up inside the lighter, the bungs would be replaced in the drain holes and on the next tide she would float.

That evening the entire party piled into cars and drove the short distance down the green lane to the creek to help Ian. There were Red Indian braves,

slave girls, pirates, and some in quite elaborate costumes. I, not given to dressing up, relied on a red pom pom sewed to the top of a beret to turn me into a French matelot and Kath resurrected an old school uniform, albeit a bit undersize, to become a St Trinian's girl. There must have been at least forty people on that lighter at high water: drunks, helpers, revellers, call them what you will, and they had all got there by the only way possible: walking along a plank from the sea wall to the lighter, and off again. It is especially memorable to me because no one fell in.

The lighter *Lillian* was ultimately to be part of the reason for my selling *Sugar Creek. Sugar* was in the lighter for some reason or other when she was seen by Chris Doyle and he made me an offer I could not refuse. I believe he had been left some money and wanted to spend it sailing to distant horizons. If you were not in a hurry, *Sugar* was the ideal boat. *Sugar's* other attraction was that she was in the *Lillian* and, as in those days sailing in blue water meant copper sheathing as defence against worm, she was in the ideal situation to do this. Chris and two friends spent the summer fitting her out. Unfortunately for his friends, Chris met a girl and when he sailed she was his only crew. Years later I saw an advertisement in a yachting magazine for a Pilot Book of the Virgin Islands. The author and publisher was given as Chris Doyle.

But before I parted with *Sugar Creek* I had a few more sails, two of which (one in winter and one in summer) could have been her last. The winter trip was to bring the boat back from Heybridge Basin on the Blackwater to Fambridge. We locked out of the basin at about midday and carried the tide down to some distance past Mersea where we anchored close in to the shore for shelter, for it was blowing fresh from the north; it was also snowing. My crew was Jimmy Green and Tony, a new neighbour of his who had never sailed before. The plan was almost a textbook navigational problem as we had done in our evening classes. We would wait for half tide, until there was water over Dengie Flats, pull up our anchor and, under reefed main, for it was blowing fresh from the north, steer south for eight miles. We would then start swinging the lead until we got into the deeper water of the mouth of the River Crouch and then alter course to southwest to get into the Crouch itself. Our intention was to find the north shore, anchor in its shelter and turn in to wait for the next flood.

It was a winter's night, black as pitch and snowing, and we did not expect to see anything en route – but there was something. During the war the

'Of course there's a funny smell and we're in it'

Dengie Flats had been used as a bombing range, originally marked with DZ buoys (dropping zone). These had been replaced by four barge hulks which were covered at high water. As I was at the helm in *Sugar*'s minute cockpit and Jimmy in the hatch, the only way Tony could see anything of the exciting new world he was being introduced to was to stand in the forward hatch. It was the few seconds' warning his startled shout gave as he saw the snow-covered sunken barge ahead that allowed me to ram the tiller over and we sluiced past it. Even if we had only started a plank in the prevailing conditions we would have been goners. Tony's first sail would have been his last.

The summer trip could have been even more disastrous as there were four of us involved. Kath, the two children and I were bound for Whitstable to visit some friends of our student days. There was a light vessel in the Swin then, the Barrow Sands, and we were just about opposite it, beating into a fresh southwesterly, when all the rigging went slack. The mast, which had just been stepped by the yard, had not been stepped completely into the keel and the movement had finally let it drop home the extra few inches. I eased

33

**'At least it shows interfacing the autopilot
with a waypoint works'**

the sheets and dropped the sails to take the strain off the mast but even
without canvas she was on a course for the Barrow Sands and the light vessel
set off a flare to warn us. To get control of *Sugar* I reset the staysail and ran
before the wind while I tightened the bottlescrews. *Sugar* had an engine but
this had the Achilles heel of many marine engines in those days – the
magneto – and it was a non starter. It was not our lucky day as, with the
shrouds set up, the mainsail tore across the leach as I was resetting it. The
wind got up considerably and the boats in the Southsea–Harwich race arrived
in the area. Enough of them got into trouble in the now gale force winds to
keep every lifeboat on the east coast busy. One yacht, as we read later in an
account published in *Yachting World*, was crewed by members of the Royal
Corp of Signals and was reported 'to be making Morse with difficulty'.

We steadily sailed through this mayhem, not that we saw any of it, as
running was the only thing I could do until somewhere in the area of the

Cutler the lights of a ship came close enough for Kath to put her Girl Guides training into use and flash out an SOS. The ship was a train ferry bound for Harwich and she came alongside to give us a lee and take us off. A rope ladder was dropped down to us from a doorway in the ferry's side, and though it was fine for Kath and myself it was hopeless for Hilary and Veronica at three and four years of age. It was a crew member who took his life in his hands and solved the problem. Two of his ship mates held him by his belt as they themselves held onto the doorway. Only in this manner could he reach down low enough to make contact with me, where I was standing on the hatch, and take one of the children from me. His remark on our first contact, for we did not always make contact, was 'Eff me, mate!' to which I replied in all sincerity 'Well, come back, there's another one.'

While this activity was going on, the rubbing strake of the ferry, which stuck out about two feet, was playing havoc with *Sugar*. The scend was such that it both knocked off the spreaders and opened up the deck and by the time I got off, the water was up to the bunks. However, this did not seem to affect the girls and we heard one tell a sympathetic sailor proudly that she had been shipwrecked, 'just like Rupert Bear'. As for *Sugar*, she kept on floating and when the weather moderated she was towed into Harwich by a Trinity House boat as a danger to navigation and was later repaired in the boatyard in Walton Backwaters. The insurance paid up and she sailed again.

# Chapter 5

## Froyna

When I parted with *Sugar Creek* I started to look for something different and as I had been crewing on Stellas in the Wednesday evening races held in Burnham I bought a Folkboat. I would have bought a Stella but as I had been pooped once in *Sugar* I could not bring myself to buy a boat without a bridge deck and a self draining cockpit. Winter was the accepted time to buy boats, when they were laid up out of the water. *Froyna* was a conventional Folkboat, clinker built with crouching headroom and she had a 10hp Sabb engine. At first I thought she was overpowered but I soon got used to it. She was lying close to us at Walton-on-the-Naze and I had arranged for her to be launched, so Jimmy Green, his neighbour Tony and I went to collect her. It was snowing when we went on board but we could not resist using the last of the daylight to find our way out to the Pye End buoy and sail into Harwich. Here we were so taken with her handiness that we took it in turns to take the tiller and pick up a buoy, which we then threw overboard and someone else took the tiller and we started again. It was when we picked up the last buoy of the evening and we went below that we truly missed *Sugar Creek. Froyna* at that time had no heating stove and she was as cold as charity below. It was like sleeping in a snowball.

**Froyna, doing what she did best: going to windward.**

We had some fabulous sails in *Froyna*, a memorable one being at Easter with three of us on board: myself, Tony and Keith, a New Zealand cartoonist who had been headhunted by a British newspaper. Keith had arrived at Fambridge straight from his office in his city suit which, as it turned out, was fortunate. The destination was initially Boulogne but in the true spirit of the Flexible Yacht Club we reacted to a fair wind from the east. Just as the old-time fishermen used to say, Easter got its name from the easterlies that blow at that time. It was fresh and fair and too good to waste – we changed our destination to Cherbourg. We ran before it, teetering on a gybe for hours. Some time on that romp down the Channel, Keith made a meal for Tony and myself which, even though we were wearing oilskins, we ate below. Keith then told us he was going to eat his meal in the cockpit. It wasn't that we had had much water on board, just the odd dollop, but it was against all our advice that he attempted to do so – it was tempting fate. He never even put his oilskins on. He had barely sat down in the cockpit with his plate on his lap when a dollop came on board. He was soaked to the skin in an instant and to this day I can still recollect seeing his plate wiped as clean as a whistle.

We arrived in Cherbourg in darkness with one thought in mind: food. Not only did we need it physically but after our 200 mile run we felt we deserved it. We entered the first restaurant we came to and it set the scene for all the others, it was packed to the rafters with ebullient yachtsmen doing what we wanted to do; eating, drinking and making merry. The wind we had run before down Channel had been a beam wind for boats from the Solent and it was Easter weekend. It seemed every yachtsman based in the Solent was now in Cherbourg. We were turned away from every restaurant we went into: none had an empty table.

We were returning to the boat and passed the first restaurant we had tried when a group of yachtsmen emerged, and that told us everything: there was an empty table inside. Even with that we were not received with open arms. The evening was almost over and I must admit we did not impress. Tony and I were alright but we looked as if we had picked up some tramp, as Keith was

'They never believe me at the office'

wearing his now creased city suit and shirt, the only dry clothes he had. In those days of detachable collars he had not considered his necessary, so his shirt was collarless and this, together with his normal heavy growth of beard looking two days heavier still, meant he was far from looking a normal yachtsman. Of the trip back from Cherbourg I can remember not one iota, but two things on the way there I will never forget. One was the plate swept clean as a whistle and second was Keith, noticeably unshaven, sitting with his jacket over the back of his chair and slowly but contentedly picking and cracking his way through a large platter of Fruits de la Mer in an empty restaurant.

In those distant days every creek had some old workboat mouldering away, and I fell for *Amy*. She was a 28ft Gravesend Bawley, she had no rudder and filled on every tide, but I fell for her. She cost me £10 with an outboard

thrown in. Jimmy Green and I caulked her with what was called Blackwall stopping (clay) and appropriated a 'Private – Keep Off' notice to use as a temporary rudder to get her back to our creek. There we made a new rudder and caulked her properly, and she did get us to Calais and back.

Her downfall was due to a lack of money and time. The lack of money was perennial and the lack of time was because I had *Froyna* to sail, so the plan to rebuild *Amy*, replacing one plank at a time, fell by the wayside. The final nail in the coffin was that the space she occupied in the dry dock was needed, so we floated her out of it, allowed her to take the ground on the saltings on a high spring tide, and I put a match to her.

Nowadays, with so many old boats being rebuilt, this seems like vandalism, but old wrecks were there for the asking back then, especially given the fact that they were considered breeding grounds for the dreaded gribble worm. To this day I have a mantelpiece made from the taffrail of the Ramsgate smack *Problem*, and I also have a steering wheel salvaged from the Thames barge *Nell Gwynn*. Only Tom Bolton's *Maria*, CK 21, was lucky enough to get a complete rebuild, and she is now one of the fastest smacks still sailing. These days I do regret the loss of *Amy*. A small traditional East Coast workboat would be ideal for my old age.

Kath and I still remember our experiences with *Froyna* in Alderney. There were five of us on board for the six weeks of the school holidays: Kath, the girls and Fred. Fred was ex Merchant Navy and he now worked at the PLA where he had been a friend of Tom Bolton. *Froyna* was tied alongside the wall in tiny Crabby Harbour on Alderney and we were all sitting in the cockpit when the bows of a boat appeared around the harbour entrance. The mast of the boat – she was big, about 50ft – was just into view when two things happened at once. A woman's voice from below shouted up, 'It's on the table!' and the boat stopped dead. Both Fred and I realised the unseen skipper had problems. The tide was away and whichever way his boat lay it was going to make contact with the harbour heads. Time was of the essence.

With Fred and I working from the harbour head on his starboard side and his crew on the port side, disaster was averted. Every halyard from the mast, the main, the topping lift, staysail, genny and spinnaker was utilised plus lines from the mast to the harbour heads. The skipper was, as I once read, very good at getting out of situations he should never have got into. At the latter stages he was using a spirit level and the boat looked like a circus tent.

However, by the time the tide had gone down enough for her to heel she was as upright as a guardsman. The skipper, as we found out, was an ex army officer who had spent his gratuity on buying the boat, *Piet Hein* (the name of a Dutch resistance fighter), in Holland. He was now running it as a charter boat and wintering in Portugal. We heard them later in the small hours when the tide returned and from the noise and laughter they made they had passed the time waiting for the tide by drinking. By the time we got up *Piet Hein* was lying alongside the harbour wall behind us.

Later that day we had been up to the town and we were approaching the harbour when we heard the squeaking noise of a rope under strain. It was easily tracked down and we went on board the deserted *Piet Hein* to ease off a masthead line, obviously put on to prevent the boat falling outwards and then forgotten. But not completely forgotten, for we were still on board when the skipper appeared on the other side of the harbour. He had obviously remembered about his masthead line when in town and had run himself into the ground to get back. When he saw us on board his boat he slumped on the ground until he got his breath back.

The last time we saw that skipper was when we were preparing to leave. We were just afloat when he and his crew appeared on the harbour wall above us. He shouted down, 'Here, catch these' and threw a large paper bag down to us. But he misjudged. The paper bag caught the spreaders and burst open, and we and the boat were showered with cream cakes. We cast off and left the harbour eating the cream horns that we could salvage and sluicing buckets of water on those we couldn't.

It was a windless day and we were under power when we heard noises we couldn't ignore coming from the engine. We didn't even bother to lift the engine cover off, so obvious was it that mending it was beyond our capabilities. It was, as we found out later, caused by a cog in the gear box that had shattered and was rattling about inside it. As we were conscious of the force of the tides in this area the obvious thing to do seemed to anchor, which we tried to do, bending every line we had on board together. We even used the main halyard by sending up a leader line so we could re-reeve it. However, as we never touched bottom and didn't have an echo sounder it made us wonder if we were over the hundred odd fathoms of the Hurd Deep where out of date explosives were dumped. We drifted for some time until a whisper of a breeze arrived from the east and we retrieved all our lines, re-

reeved them and started heading north. We crept into Weymouth as dawn was breaking. It was drizzling and was, at 38 hours, our longest ever Channel crossing. The engineer who repaired the engine was a lifeboat mechanic, and a remark he made has influenced me over the years: 'Small diesels and big filters have knocked the bottom out of the lifeboat business.' I've had big filters ever since.

We obviously used the repaired engine to help us further west and into Torquay – where I was put to shame. It was a windless day and we had motored up to a mooring buoy as the club secretary rowed out to greet us as they often did in those distant days. He asked where we had come from and I replied 'Essex', which seemed a reasonable distance away. He then inquired 'What club are you from?' and we both looked up at the burgee where it hung limp at the masthead. Almost on cue on that completely windless day, a puff of wind arrived, not much but just enough, and my burgee stretched out long enough for the word 'Heineken' to be read. I felt it was pointless my trying to excuse myself by saying it had taken a 160 mile round trip across the North Sea to get that burgee. I also feel guilty that I probably helped the demise of the very civilised custom of yacht club secretaries rowing out to welcome visiting yachts.

Torquay must have been on the last leg of our cruise. With the children on board we often sailed at night and our return to the east started at night – in fact, at closing time. We were leaving Torquay as the liberty boats from a naval ship that was anchored in the bay were returning with their, I have no doubt, inebriated crews. They were singing and in fine voice; drunk they may have been and perhaps it was distance that gave that extra something to their voices, but it was memorable. The song they were singing was a very appropriate folk tune and one we knew well: 'When our money is all spent we'll go to sea once more.'

One of the last sails we had in *Froyna* also had folk song connotations. When we had *Froyna* we often sailed in company with *Thyatira* for they had about the same performance. On this occasion we were tied up alongside each other in Boulogne harbour, Ian with Jimmy Green as crew and I had Kath and the two girls, and there were about six French boats sharing the only pontoon. Kath assures me it was two in the morning and she was getting worried at our non return until she heard voices singing in the distance – drunken voices. Where we went wrong was in not getting straight

into our bunks and instead, once back on board, Ian pulling out his squeeze box. He also chose the wrong tune: 'The Bargemen's Alphabet'. It actually has 26 verses but Ian couldn't remember what Q stood for. 'Q is for the quarter deck where the skipper do walk' completely jumped his mind, but instead of simply missing it out he started again from 'A is for the anchor that we carry on the bows', plus the chorus. He did this a number of times as the French boats gradually departed. It all ended when Ian, who was giving this solo act leaning over his boom with his feet dangling in the air, leant too far forward. Gravity took over and he fell into the bottom of his cockpit and more or less knocked himself out. When we got up in the morning *Thyatira* had gone. Ian had woken up during the night and being ashamed of his antics (as a head-master should be) and probably conscious of why the French had left, he decided to go quietly. But he has never been allowed to forget it.

It was probably feeling I needed more space on board that led to my parting with *Froyna*, though she didn't move far. In fact, she kept the same mooring at Fambridge and her new owner, David Ellis, an anaesthetist at the Royal College of Surgeons, fitted into the Flexible Yacht Club in the manner born. Then followed what a few of us considered the ideal way of passing the winter weekends: looking for another boat. In those days boatyards closed on Fridays in the winter and the usual procedure was to ring the yard and find where the boat you were interested in was shored up. You would gener-ally get some description such as 'she has a green cover and is behind the crane at the end of the yard'. So off three or four of you would go on a Saturday morning, with a list of the boats you were interested in and where to find them. We would track them down in the deserted boatyards, crawl all over them, and on the Saturday evening we would hopefully find a B&B in some convenient pub where we could eat and drink and discuss our findings of the day.

# Chapter 6
## Dowsabel

We found *Dowsabel* in a canal off the River Humber. She was what you could term a pretty boat, a 33ft yawl with fine lines, attractive sheer and a neat canoe stern. The owner, who had never sailed, had been planning a long voyage until his wife put her foot down about the cost. The owner before him had hinted that it was his own design but when I found out that his neighbour had been the yacht designer Francis B Jones, and judging by what my own eyes told me, I did not worry on that score. Someone had done their sums right.

There was a 18hp belt-driven Saab diesel fitted, and the prop ran under the engine, driven by four V belts. I often wondered why this method was not more common. If you caught anything around your prop, the belts squealed but no damage was done and it gave you time to switch the engine off. You didn't have to be so exact in lining the engine up and although I carried spare belts I only used one once. She had a smallish well drained cockpit and this helped to compensate for the only major fault I found in her – the canoe stern. I was pooped twice in her. What I never expected on these occasions, but I assure you it happens, is that as you sit in a cockpit full of water, the water climbs up the inside of your oilskins to your crotch in

**Dowsabel becalmed.**

seconds. However, it only happened twice. She was fitted with two alloy spars and square sails for running down the trades. I now regret I never tried them out, but in simplifying the halyards I got rid of the hoists and guys. Fortunately she also had a coal stove fitted, as we took her away in the winter.

On one of our first sails in *Dowsabel* we met the man who said he had designed her. It was during the school holidays and Ian Griffiths and I had worked the boat down to the Solent, planning a holiday of fair winds home with the prevailing south westerlies. There were six of us on board: Kath and the two girls, Ian and June (his new New Zealand wife) and myself. I knew that the first owner of *Dowsabel* lived in Guernsey, and that he was a doctor who had fled the NHS. We made contact and were invited to meet him. His house had a marvellous view overlooking the harbour, and sculls on the wall told us he had rowed for his college. All we had in common was *Dowsabel* and even there we were different. He was old fashioned enough to think that the pushpit and pulpit she now had would ruin her lines and he hinted that they were slightly wimpish. I have no doubt that his glasses were on us as we left the harbour.

Our theory about fair winds home proved correct but it was our visit to Isigny that provided the highlight of the holiday. We were the first yacht into Isigny that year and Ian and I, who had become friendly with a couple of the fishermen, were asked if we'd like to go out fishing with them. Isigny is a drying harbour and fishermen have to work the tides, so our stint started as a night trip. We were fishing for mussels. It was probably the hardest work we had done in years.

We were fishing from smallish open boats about 26ft long in the shallow waters east of the Cherbourg peninsula and the method was primitive. We used long rakes with handles 20–30ft long, and tines of about 18in. We threw the head of the rakes out and pulled them back in. Once they were underneath the boat you brought the head of the rake, now heavy and full of rock, shell, seaweed and hopefully mussels, hand over hand to the surface and levered it on board. After you had picked out the mussels you repeated the procedure ad infinitum. As I said, it was hard work and that night it was harder still, for even our French friends told us it was a phenomenal catch. We were loaded to the gun'ls and even borrowed sacks off the other boats to fill with our catch, as the fishermen had to play out this lucky strike. Whether it was the extra two rakes or just luck, but either way we could do no wrong that night in Isigny. We were looked on as lucky charms.

We were in *Dowsabel* when the Flexible Yacht Club reached its zenith. It had been discussed and agreed that the Channel Islands would be the destination of the club during the summer holiday. The exact timing was left to the individuals but that was where we were bound and notes would be left with the Harbourmaster at Alderney when each boat arrived. I set off with Keith the New Zealander, who now had an East Anglian. We were close together on a fresh beam reach as we came out of the shelter of the North Foreland. His actions said what I was thinking, his arm stabbing to the northeast. I was close enough to hear the odd word and two were enough: 'Dutch Pete'. Dutch Pete was a Dutch cruising man who had turned up in Fambridge just in time to receive an invitation to one of Jimmy's parties. Before he left he had said, 'If you ever come to Helevetsluis you will be welcome'. So, in the best tradition of the club, we eased our sheets and ran northeast. As we locked into Helevetsluis we could see over the lock gates four burgees advertising Heineken beers. Only *Gladys*, with her powerful diesel, got to Alderney.

The timing of our arrival in Helevetsluis was impeccable; it was the day of the local club's regatta and – no doubt at Dutch Pete's instigation – we were invited to join in. What's more it was a special regatta. The Haring Fleet was open to the sea but a few days later it was to be cut off and have a lock. It would be the last time the local cruising boats would go out to sea on a race. The Flexible Yacht Club won enough to embarrass us at the prizegiving, and that I think was the highest peak the club ever reached.

It was in *Dowsabel* that I first got into taking out charter parties. This came about in a very casual manner for, as I had sailed down the Crouch on a Friday evening, I had often been hailed by the skipper of a large, slab sided, beamy, gaff cutter, called *Dorothea*. She was on the only mooring in Cliff Reach and the skipper always seemed to be rowing people out to it and his

**Fishing off Isigny – one of the highlights of our holiday.**

greeting was always the same: 'Where are you bound?' I always felt I should be replying the 'Indies' or 'Trincomalee' or some such romantic destination instead of the Medway or Heybridge Basin. I found out he was a civil servant and the people he was rowing aboard were members of the Civil Servants' Sailing Association. Chartering was a sideline of his. He liked sailing and it paid for the boat. And that is how I started taking out his latest crew. He gave me some instructions which would make life easier for him in the future, when they would be sailing on *Dorothea*: I had to teach them how to put a reef in, tie a bowline and light the Primus. It was some time afterwards that he was transferred to the south coast and I never saw him, or *Dorothea*, or members of the Civil Servants' Sailing Association, again. But I had learnt that chartering could be a good thing.

# Chapter 7

## Concerto

I rather unexpectedly became the owner of another boat. She was a Vertue called *Concerto*. Vertues are now considered classics but then they were simply considered a good quality wooden boat, depending on who had built them. Her owner, known to all as Scotch Bob, was a slightly-built character with a soft Scottish burr and had his mate's ticket in the Merchant Navy. In the winter he went to sea, hopefully on voyages to warmer climes, and in summer he sailed the east coast in *Concerto*. Fambridge was his base because his sister, who was his only living relative, had married a man in a nearby village. It was when Scotch Bob was away at sea there was a fire in the shed at the boatyard and *Concerto*'s hull was badly damaged. Fate was not finished with Bob, for his sister then died suddenly. Among her effects was the unopened reminder from his insurance company to renew the premium on *Concerto*. Not only had Bob lost his only living relative but he had lost his boat as well, for she was uninsured. The only thing I could think of to help Bob, for he was going back to sea, was to buy *Concerto* as she stood on his valuation, have her repaired and sell her. If there was any profit we would share it.

With *Concerto* repaired, I became a two-boat owner and I was spoiled for choice for she was a pleasure to sail but, at 25ft narrow and, to me, deep, not

a boat to charter with. I think she was sold over the phone when a buyer heard the full story and I offered to deliver her to the Solent. And here I was hoisted by my own petard.

The only piece of gear I had taken out of her was the small heating stove, which was a little beauty. It had fins on the side so that the convected heat was out of all proportion to her size. We had reached the Downs on the delivery trip when the wind

Concerto after the fire.

freshened from the southwest and we anchored for shelter. We were not alone, as five or six coasters were also there, and then it became cold, colder and then started to snow, but all was not lost for the wind went around to the north and the Downs emptied. We were well on our way down Channel when I got a cartoon idea handed to me, as the saying has it, on a plate. I was on watch, convinced my relief had overslept, when the hatch slid back and a muffled figure appeared. He glanced around and took in the surroundings: the darkness, the swirling snow flakes, the bitterly cold north wind, the only sign of man being the flash of the Beachy Head light. 'D'you know, Mike, there's times when sailing is only a leetle bit better than work.' Later I drew it straight.

With the purchase price in hand there was money to pass on to Bob – but where was Bob? Eventually he turned up at our cottage and my offer of his share of the money was refused. The insurance company, The East Coast Mutual, had heard the sad story and paid up in full. The company itself was one where you could only be invited to become a member on the recommendation of other members.

Having decided that getting paid for doing something you enjoyed was a good idea, I decided that I would take up chartering myself. But it had its snags. I also discovered that there was very little money to be made out of it. However, that was compensated for me by the fact that I was now selling cartoons to yachting magazines all over the world, even to Japan, and char-

**'Sometimes, Mike, sailing is only a little bit better than work'**

terers, if nothing else, provided the ideas and all I had to do was draw them. It also had other repercussions. One was that you never sailed with your friends. I saw their boats sailing, we crossed tacks at times but that was it, we never met as we had in the past. I made many other friends, but they were spread all over the country and our meetings were sporadic.

When I started chartering I put three ads in magazines, the only three I have ever put in, to advertise my charter weekends. Looking back on them now tells me a lot of what I hoped for. One was in *Yachting Monthly*, another in *The Scout* and another in *The Spectator*, all magazines I had worked for. What I now realise I was hoping for was a composite charterer, one with his own oilskins, who knew which way to push the tiller, lively and active with an interesting line of conversation when we were at anchor.

I got some strange mixtures but this was probably my own doing. My ad in *The Spectator* started, 'Wind on the cheek, brother, or sister, how long since...?' One woman turned up from Hampstead, and would have taken out a season ticket as she realised she could have a captive audience of four or

five men every weekend. The Rover Scouts, all in their late teens or early twenties, were a fantastic crowd, nothing fazed them, but they got older and got married. One, Gary Pritchard, with a mordant sense of humour, ended up as a lecturer in a German university and recommended me to some of his more blasé students. He hoped for the worst the east coast could offer, and his hopes were more than realised. But his students rose to the occasion and went back full of enthusiasm for the experience.

I was with Gary the only time I went for the liferaft in earnest. We were over the Ostende Bank and it was one of the times I had been pooped in *Dowsabel*. I was below making sandwiches at the time when water came pouring in over the top of the washboards and I had to put my hand on Gary's face to push him back as he tried to come below. When it was all straightened out I asked him why he had wanted to come below. He told me with a grin that he could see the tower blocks of Ostende and he wanted the flippers in his bag.

PEYTON

'When I pull you off, pull up the main, let out the jib
and sheet them both in, then push the tiller towards me
and pick me up as you sail by'

However, it was the members of dinghy clubs that made the best charterers. I still sail with some of the first who volunteered over thirty years ago, from Frampton SC in Gloucester, and from Sparkhill SC in the Midlands, and some from Crewe Engine Sheds. I still use the oblong frying pan they made for me. It is beautifully made of heavy gauge copper and fits the top of my stove to the millimetre.

PEYTON

'It's an electronic voice saying
"leave your message after the tone"'

# Chapter 8

## Lodestone

Although I was happy sailing and chartering with *Dowsabel*, I soon realised that a larger boat would give better returns for little extra outlay. But I was quite content to continue with her – until I saw a ferro cement boat being built. Immediately I realised what the economies could be with this method of construction, but even more attractive was the realisation that I could have a boat built to my own ideas. With GRP I would have to accept a design, even if I could afford it. With a wooden boat the cost would be prohibitive but with ferro I could afford it. I decided that 40ft would be the ideal length as I was confident I could handle a boat of this size alone if necessary and I could fit eight berths in it. I went to a boat show and went on board every forty footer there looking for ideas, and was disappointed. One I remember was advertised as having an interior by an 'international designer' and I went on board with high hopes. However, his designs seemed to be based around large colourful scatter cushions. Scatter cushions and wet oilskins?

I ended up with the ideas and a rough plan of a boat which I realised was a composite of all the best bits of the boats I had previously owned. The boat I had seen being built was being constructed by Ferro Marine Services of Burnham and it was from them I learnt that Alan Hill, a local yacht designer,

**'Having second thoughts?'**

was one of the few who had been broad minded enough to accept commissions for ferro construction. Many yacht designers thought ferro was beneath them. So it was to Alan Hill I went with my ideas for a basic shallow draught sea going boat.

I doubt if I could have gone to anyone better. Alan was an enthusiast. We had our arguments but as we were both after the same thing (a good seaworthy boat), we solved them together and finished good friends and the end result, *Lodestone*, was a winner.

I had always liked *Sugar Creek*'s small cockpit, on the assumption that in bad weather a cockpit cannot be small enough, and in good weather who cares? So I went for a smallish cockpit. The cockpit drains were ample, two 8in x 2in holes going directly through a buoyant transom, which had a stern hung rudder. I went for a flush deck of glass over ply as on *Dowsabel*. I had known the misery of deck leaks in the past. This one had a 10in camber, so water did not linger long. The doghouse had a chart table big enough to take an Admiralty chart. Underneath the chart table was an easily accessible air cooled 44hp Lister diesel, with a hand start. A charterer who used Listers in his construction business described them truthfully as Paddy proof. Because she was shoal draught with hardly any bilges I was regretfully unable to use a belt drive system. The shoal draught, 4ft, was possible because of a centre-board which was out of sight under the saloon table. She could sleep eight: two in quarter berths and two in the forepeak with three berths in the saloon. One, which was very popular, was a pilot berth, and I had my own berth in the doghouse alongside the chart table close to the cockpit. *Lodestone* was yawl rigged, as I had found with chartering the more bits of string to pull the better.

She was labour intensive and the mizzen staysail was used a lot. She had no echo sounder and a lead was swung when needed. I had noticed that parties (which sometimes took place when we were tied alongside other boats) always took place in the biggest cabin available, so I tried to keep this space free. The cabin was 11ft x 11ft and over the years it saw its share of parties. It also had a coal stove fitted, which made all the difference in wet weather and on night passages. Ultimately I was sailing weekends in winter as well as summer and the stove seldom went out. I think some of my regulars would have come on Christmas Day if I had allowed them.

As I was against putting holes in the hull on principle, I initially had a

One of our traditional Christmas sails. Kath fourth from the right, Mike third.

bucket and chuck it for the toilet arrangements and then after pressure from some of the punters, friends and Kath (especially Kath), I moved to an Elsan. But that was still unacceptable so holes were finally drilled in the hull and a toilet fitted.

The mast was stepped on deck in a tabernacle and incorporated an idea I had seen on a Dutch boat where the mast could be lowered without easing the cap shrouds, so it was

always under control. She had only two second hand winches for the large headsail, a Christmas present from Kath. There were complaints about the lack of an anchor winch but I found four or five willing charterers could always get the anchor up. I also found for all their complaints they kept coming back, year after year, some of them for over 30 years. I worked on the principle of keeping the boat moving, following Nelson's dictum 'Men and ships rot in harbour'.

It was these ideas that Alan Hill put down on paper and then all one had to do was to transfer them into something concrete. The early seventies were a fantastic time to be building in ferro, it truly was the flavour of the month. But if it had its pros it also had its cons. Forty foot became the average size for a ferro boat. Smaller than that and it was heavy, larger and the costs went up. With the design chosen from a book, and using cheap materials of iron bar, chicken wire, sand and cement and your own labour, hundreds of hulls must have been built. But the hull was approximately only a third of the cost of the boat. Many builders failed to make costings of everything else needed – engine, spars, sails, etc. And 4oft is a big boat. Nevertheless it was a brilliant time to build one. Besides myself, Jimmy Green, Ian Griffiths and Mick the Brick were also building ferro boats. Jimmy Green built his to accommodate a glassfibre hull and deck he had acquired. Ian Griffiths built big and ultimately took crews on the Tall Ships races, whereas Mick the Brick became the acknowledged expert in the manner of construction.

**Lodestone takes shape.**

**Plastering day – the day a rather large birdcage becomes a hull.**

We met other builders when it came to plastering days, the day when the cheap but labour intensive mesh of metal and wire had the cement applied. This was a one-shot operation and plenty of labour was required. This worked on the premise 'I'll help you and you help me.' I went to some marvellous plastering days. The weather was always good – it had to be or the job was cancelled. The cement mixer (and there was always a standby mixer) started at about nine and the work commenced. The labour was to transfer about ten tonnes of cement in buckets up to the wired up hull. Inside the hull, willing hands pushed it out through the mesh. Outside, the

only people being paid for their work applied their skill as plasterers to see it did not go too far. All the time this work was going on the women saw to it that there was food (invariably bacon or fried egg sandwiches) and mugs of tea available on tap. Come mid afternoon, things were slowing down and plastering day took on another connotation, as beer took over from tea as a thirst quencher. I am sure all builders of ferro boats went to marvellous plastering days like these.

When the boats were being wired up there was always a stream of visitors who were thinking of building one and wanted to see it in progress. One Saturday morning when *Lodestone* was being built in the garden behind the house, Kath's record of the cups of coffee she supplied was 24.

With the hull completed, the engine was installed and the main bulkheads fitted. *Lodestone* was decked over, with material below for finishing off the interior. Shortly after that she was launched and rigged and on her way to Calais. The crew were Kath and the girls (for it was school holidays) and a friend of mine, Vic Temple. Vic was the type of man who could turn his hand to anything. At the time he was building a Wharran catamaran and later he and his German wife Lina (who he met while in the army of occupation) sailed away to distant horizons. He financed his way of life by buying a plot of land wherever he was, building a house on it, selling it and sailing on. Now he was giving me a hand down to the Med for friendship's sake and because such interludes appealed to him, especially the idea that we fitted the boat out as we went along (which surprisingly didn't appeal to Kath).

We lowered the mast at Calais, which was easier said than done as there was only provision for lowering dinghy masts there and *Lodestone's* main mast was 44ft. Because the new mizzen sail hadn't arrived before we left the Crouch the mizzen mast hadn't been stepped so *Lodestone* was sloop rigged and we only had the main mast to contend with. To do this we moored the boat in the corner of the harbour with her bows tight against the harbour wall, then with a masthead line tied to a massive bollard we waited for low water and, with one of us surging from above, we successfully lowered away. Having a mast in a tabernacle and the pick up point for the cap shrouds in line with the mast bolt in the tabernacle was paying off. The other absolutely essential task we did at Calais was to collect our *Carte Verte*. This certificate of bureaucracy, which was free, was to see us through approximately 200 locks in France on our near 800 mile journey to the Med. Our last under-

**Lodestone the day before launching**

taking before we locked into the Canal du Nord was to empty the forepeak of its cargo of scooter tyres, the fenders of the impecunious yachtsman of the day, and make a necklace of these to thread all around the boat. With a French courtesy flag fluttering from a makeshift flag staff, the voyage into the interior commenced.

It was the start of a trip of continual interest in many respects. France at that time was in political turmoil, with governments coming and going as if in a revolving door. Two fishing boats tied alongside each other in Calais summed it up. One was called *Madonna of the Sea,* the other *Karl Marx.* These divisions affected the lock-keepers, some treating you like a bloated plutocrat,

'He's out, working on his boat'

others as the reason for their job. No longer a sinecure for wounded ex-soldiers, some locks had political slogans painted on them, others hand-painted signs telling you they had eggs for sale. Even the coal fields of northern France provided interest for us, as they had been the battlefields of the 1914–18 war and we went along canals that had been the front line, with the opposing forces on opposite banks. In Compiègne we found an impressive museum devoted to the various types of boats found on the inland waterways of France. This I found interesting, particularly the section devoted to the River Rhône, as we ourselves would be going down it and at that time it didn't have a very good reputation. However, that was in the future.

Another point of interest was the Bony Tunnel. Built by Austrian prisoners of war in Napoleonic days, it was almost 7km long and we were towed through it by electric motor at the tail end of a line of 21 barges at less than 1 mile an hour. In fact, we spent the night in it asleep. As I had also been involved in building a tunnel while a prisoner of war I could identify myself with the Austrians – the damp, the darkness, the depression. Though, unlike them, hundreds of miles from home and with escape impossible, my escape route had been a short one, to the advancing Russian army, where now with a carbine in my hand, I was able to turn around and settle some scores.

As always, Paris had plenty to offer and one cannot live much more centrally in Paris than on the Quai d'Orsay. The Eiffel Tower was but a stone's throw away, along with the Louvre, Notre Dame and just about all of Paris itself. It was in Paris that we parted from Kath and the girls as the school holidays were over. They were returning home as Vic and I turned south through the Nivernais Canal to join the River Rhône.

By now, almost imperceptibly, I was becoming a professional yachtsman for, not only was I regularly selling cartoons and the occasional photograph to yachting magazines but I was also selling articles to them. In fact, the few I have left have provided invaluable aide memoires to this book, I only wish I had more. One short feature that was published was of the variety of the people who acknowledged our waves. I got the idea when we were passing a prison. I could see this pale face watching our passing from a small barred window and I waved towards it. To that watcher we must have seemed the epitome of freedom: two tanned, shirtless young travellers heading south without a care in the world. His reply was muted. We also waved to two nuns who were walking soberly and demurely along the canal path. They looked all around them to see if they were being observed, then at each other as if to agree, then replied to our waves enthusiastically. One evening we waved to an old woman closing a shutter. She hesitated, then a timid movement of her hand and the shutter closed. Some of the most enthusiastic replies we received were from the village women as they did their washing in the canal. I doubt if they do it nowadays, but then they scrubbed and rinsed and gossiped and seemed glad of a break in their normal routine.

There was one wave that wasn't a wave as such but said a lot more. We were passing a factory and it was lunch time, a lively and colourful scene with scores of workers all dressed alike in red overalls and peaked caps. Our waves were returned a hundredfold. Some pointed to themselves and then the boat, signifying could they come with us? Then their calls were left behind. We were at least half a kilometre from the factory when we got the last acknowledgement to a wave. It came from a solitary figure laid in the

long grass on the canal bank. He also wore a bright red overall with his red cap tipped over his eyes, but if his overalls signified he was with them, he was not of them. His hands were behind his head and one leg was crossed over the other, he could have been asleep. Tentatively I raised a hand towards him; at first no sign came from the recumbent figure, then I saw the slightest movement of his foot, perhaps an inch or two up and an inch or two down, and then we had passed and he was gone, but never forgotten.

It was on this stretch that I thought I was going to lose my boat and this traumatic experience was caused in the most unexpected manner. Some of the locks were now electronically controlled; no *eclusier*, or lock-keeper, to sell you eggs, honey, goats' cheese, rhubarb jam, or vegetables; simply a metal ring to pull as you entered the lock. Then the gates closed behind you and you sank down to the bottom of the lock, then as the lower gates opened and you engined out you broke an electronic ray and after a short interval the gate closed behind you. No longer were the gates the ancient leaking wooden ones you had to put your backs to in order to operate but massive steel ones that slid out of the lock walls.

In this particular case it was a flight of locks dropping down the slope with a village street running alongside. As we entered the first lock Vic saw the *boulangerie*, and we needed bread. With a brief word of explanation to me as to where he was going, he stepped onto the lockside as the boat sank down and crossed the street to the *boulangerie*. It was a few minutes later, as the lock gates opened to let *Lodestone* out, that things went wrong. As the gates opened I saw an arm appear ahead of me, as if out of the wall, waving a long French loaf. There were steps let into the wall outside the lock and Vic was letting me know he was at the bottom of them.

What neither of us realised then was that an electronic ray cannot differentiate between a French baguette and a 40ft boat. It reacts the same. *Lodestone* had barely got her bows out of the lock when the steel gates, which we estimated to be 35ft by 2ft, started to close silently and inexorably. Contact was made amidships and I was so sure that this was the end for *Lodestone* that I ran to the bows so that I would be outside the lock chamber when she sank. Bells rang and lights flashed and though *Lodestone* was firmly held as if in a huge vice, no damage was done to her. Twenty minutes later the emergency services arrived in a small van with corrugated bodywork (which the French called flying dustbins) and all was resolved, no questions asked.

We sailed on to Lyons where we were stopped for a completely different reason: an industrial strike. We were fortunate in that if one was going to be held up, Lyons, the second city in France, is as good a place to be held up as anywhere, but held up we were. It was a strike of bargees and the way they made their case seemed pointless. They blocked the River Rhône, as it now was, from bank to bank by lashing their barges together to make a barrage. As they themselves were the only people who used the waterways commercially, the only people who were inconvenienced were themselves along with a few others such as myself. Here, time ran out for Vic and he left me. Though we wrote to each other occasionally I didn't see him again for years, until his luck ran out in Maine. He had bought some acres of forest and was building a cabin there when he got a tumour on his brain. As he had always kept up his National Insurance wherever he was, he returned to England and the NHS. We always met when I sailed into Harwich and he was very philosophical about his problem saying 'We've all got to go sometime and I've had a marvellous life.'

Because of the bargees' strike there were five boats held up, tied to the elegant quays at Lyon, a Swiss, a Belgian and three British. On one small boat, there was a cramped crew of four New Zealanders. It was with these crews that *Lodestone* held her first party. Our conversation always revolved around two things: the bargees' strike and whether one should take a pilot

'Yes that's it, fully comprehensive cover...
creditcard number 68059...'

down the Rhône. We had all heard or read horror stories of boats going aground in the Rhône and having to stay there until melting snow in the distant Alps raised the water level many months later. The reason we debated this was because the Rhône Pilots were expensive, and at times obligatory, and as yacht owners we were, almost to a man, living on a shoe-string. But wine was cheap and we were young. *Lodestone* found me new friends in Lyons.

France also had people building boats in ferro and the word soon got around that there was 'un Anglais ferro ciment bateau sur la quai'. It usually started with a tapping on the hull and after I had showed these tappers over *Lodestone* it invariably ended with them taking me to see what they were building. I became particularly friendly with Henri who was building a ferro hull in the grounds of an old chateau. It was his partner Marie who was the instigator of another party, which I think could only happen in France. I think it was the local press who started it off. They pointed out to the striking bargees that we, who had been interviewed by the press and had done the bargees no harm, were the ones that were suffering the most inconvenience. The message went home and an answer came back via the local press: a barge would be withdrawn from the line of barges at a specific time and our five boats would be allowed to go through. I asked Henri if he would like to accompany me down the Rhône a few miles and catch a bus back but he could not get time off work, but Marie, and a friend of hers, could. In fact they were highly delighted.

On the whole our leaving the quai at Lyons was a very jolly occasion. We cast off, waved to the regular dog walkers who we had got to know and assembled in a flotilla for the few miles down to the line of barges. The press were waiting there with cameras and the two barges that we had to go between were choc-a-bloc with cheering bargees. We even got a memento, a small salver with the arms of the Bargees Union on it, and Marie showed me it was for tasting wine.

'It looks as if we'll just have to relax for a couple
of hours, dear, until low water'

It was as we were swooshing down the Rhône a couple of hours later that Marie signified to slow down and tie up alongside an ancient stone quay on the starboard bank. Immediately opposite it, in fact the only building there, was a small restaurant. In sign language she told me we were going to eat. Our arrival had been observed through the open door and windows and as we entered we were the cynosure of the few diners there as Marie spoke to the waiter. Everything ended in smiles and to my surprise we returned to *Lodestone*. We were followed shortly afterwards by the waiter who spread the ubiquitous paper tablecloth on the saloon table and laid out the cutlery, plates and glasses. Seemingly we were eating on board, as Marie was so taken with the novelty of being on a boat that she did not see why she should fritter it away and eat ashore when the restaurant was so convenient. Both waiters seemed delighted with the change in their routine and took it in turns to serve us.

By the time we reached the coffee stage everyone in the restaurant had moved on board to have a closer look at *le bateau Anglais*. With hindsight I think this must have been an open invitation from Marie which had been passed on by the waiters, Marie explaining things to them as if she had been at sea all her life. With a stiff arm she demonstrated the use of the hand bearing compass, she swung the lead and had the parallel ruler marching over the chart table in fine style. All the things I had previously shown her in reply to her queries were now re-enacted. She had a captive audience in the crowded cabin and it was a party of a kind, even if the host couldn't communicate with any of his guests.

Later that afternoon we arrived at the Lock Bollène, then – and it may still be – the deepest lock in Europe. As our four companions from Lyons had already passed through, *Lodestone* entered this huge lock in solitary splendour. I felt guilty about the massive amount of water that needed to be displaced to lock me through and blessed the *Carte Verte* that made it possible. It was shortly after this that Marie and her friend jumped ship and I continued on down alone. I was through Port Saint Louis when I saw a mound of scooter tyres on the bank and realised my trip through France had finished. It had been an interesting journey but *Lodestone* was a sailing boat and had been motoring too long; I felt as a bird must feel when let out of its cage.

Now all I had to do was to get the mast up. It was a tree that decided it all. It had to be near the water, easy to climb and strong, and by chance when

I found it I had an audience, who turned out to be essential. It took much longer to do this than to write it but first I put the bows of *Lodestone* into the bank opposite the tree and made her fast to it, then I rowed out the two anchors, main and kedge, from her quarters and winched them home; she was now secure at right angles to the bank.

**Lodestone in home waters sailing down the Wallet.**

The next job was to slide the mast back to the tabernacle where I could slide the bolt through the foot of the tabernacle, then climb the tree. This was a complicated procedure as I had to make the mainsheet block as high up as I thought feasible and then lead a masthead line through it. This latter part was complicated as branches kept getting in the way, but eventually, with the rope in my hand and standing at the foot of the tree, I turned to my audience. There were about eight fishermen, who had been watching me with interest for hours and I now shook the end of the rope at them. To a man, they left their rods and came over to me grinning. With them hauling on the rope and with the backstay and cap shrouds already set up with me on the foredeck ready to fasten the forestay to the stem head as soon as it was possible, it was over in minutes and *Lodestone* was a sailing boat again.

I set off eastwards along the coast across the Gulf of Fos and soon worked out for myself what I later heard referred to as the Mediterranean rig: mainsail and motor, and the mainsail was to keep some shade on the deck. Though the Med has some vicious weather at times, memory tells me I averaged one sailing day in three. A disadvantage of this from my point of view was that my idea of keeping things simple meant that my engine was air cooled, with no water pump and apertures in the hull. This might be ideal in the UK where a little heat seldom comes amiss, but in the Med it had its drawbacks. One thing that did appal me was the litter. I especially recall approaching Marseilles, where I motored over a calm windless sea through the seemingly endless detritus of the city. With no tide to carry it away, any rubbish that could float simply floated and stayed there.

However, the sun was shining and I hadn't yet reached Marseilles. I came across marinas for the first time but I was soon shown how to make the most of them by the few English-speaking birds of passage I met. The marinas only charged you if you stayed overnight, so you made use of this oversight of theirs by going in the marina and tying up while you did your shopping or sightseeing, then went out to anchor off. It was a regular occurrence at that time with yachts flying the red ensign arriving at anchorages as yachts flying the tricolour left.

These sailing vagabonds also introduced me to what they called 'chateau plastic'. I was told that every town or village had a farmers' cooperative where you could buy wine at a ridiculously low price. You were expected to take your own container, generally a five litre plastic one, hence the name.

As it was looked on as a thirst quencher, the wine was watered down to taste and sugar lumps added. It was something one could get addicted to and many did.

One of these seaborne vagabonds also told me I must anchor off the Ile de Porquerolles and explore it. His description was so apt it is fresh in my mind to this day. He extended his arms in front of him and hooked his two thumbs together, with the remark 'There are butterflies as big as this' and he flapped the palms of his hands as if they were the wings of a butterfly. With a description as visual as this I felt I must go and have a look.

Though I did see largish butterflies I have another more vivid memory of the Ile de Porquerolles, now with three marinas I believe. The day I anchored off it was deserted except for one other small British yacht. I was rowing ashore when I heard piercing shrieks and shortly afterwards an attractive young woman wearing the rig of the day for women, a tiny bikini, came running onto the beach as fast as her legs would carry her and made for her partner, who was working on their dinghy. Her excited explanation obviously didn't impress him because I heard him laughing. I was curious and

walked in the direction she had come from and after a time I came to the cause of her alarm. There were at least a couple of hundred of them, all very brown, mostly bearded, very hairy and very masculine and there wasn't a stitch of clothing between the lot of them. Perhaps her shrieks had been because her imagination had told her of the potential danger.

'Must have his partner down'

It was in this area that I was invited to a launching party more or less as the guest of honour. I say guest of honour because I was the first English ferro boat that had sailed in the area. The invititation was from Les Frères de la Mer, the Brothers of the Sea, a group of enthusiasts who had banded together and formed a commune to build 12 ferro boats. All the hulls, which were identical, were now finished. The first was to be launched and I was invited. They had been built in a clump of palm trees that ran down to the beach and on the evening prior to the launching I anchored off. When I rowed ashore to the encampment, for there was no other word to describe it with its basic shelters and cooking fires, the finished hulls were stood grey and elephant-like under the palms. The atmosphere was electric as the culmination of months of work and the realisation of their dreams drew nigh but it all turned to ashes. As the first hull entered the water she went down by the head. It was a disaster, a major design fault, and all knew there were 11 more ashore built to the same design. I left them in their misery.

It was as I worked my way eastwards that I realised I was becoming part of a loosely structured English-speaking group. It was small enough for them all to know about each other, and as the boats criss-crossed from harbour to harbour the news and gossip went with them. You would see a boat for the first time yet know everything about the skipper and his crew and their circumstances, and they did about you. My own coming was known about because the boats that I had left Lyons with had preceded me. Moreover, most harbours had an area where it was free to tie up and this area was invariably where this group was to be found. There was usually a convenient bar they considered theirs as well. It was very pleasant to go into a harbour for the first time and find that the person who took your lines recognised your boat and knew your name. You also knew that there would be a bar close by, and kindred spirits.

In St Tropez (then famous because Bridget Bardot lived there) I caught up with one of my friends from Lyons. He had delivered a boat there and was now skipper cum paid hand for the owner. He had found himself a girlfriend who followed the lead given by Bridget Bardot and went about topless. She was on board *Lodestone* with another friend following the same fashion when Kath arrived. As Kath told me later, it was quite a surprise. Another feature of this fashion for going topless was that it was considered de rigueur to wear a German Iron Cross as a necklace. It was obvious a pendant would have lain comfortably there but fashion decreed that an Iron Cross it had to be, which was the least likely decoration to lie easy in such moorings. I thought at the time that it probably had some deep psychological meaning for the French to use Germany's highest award for military valour for such a trivial purpose.

With Kath, Hilary and Veronica now on board for the school holidays we went along the coast to Cannes and laid a course for Calvi in Corsica – a trip of about a hundred miles. To make life easier I picked up another crew member. Ed was a Canadian I'd met in the bar where all these seaborne wanderers and drifters seemed to find their way. Ed was a lawyer who had not practised. He told me he had just finished his legal studies when he was involved in a car accident. He had successfully conducted his own case and, what was more to the point, he had written a book on how to do it. Though

not a bestseller, it had made him enough money for him to think about a long break and he decided to visit Japan. I wanted an extra crew for the trip to Corsica and the way he was travelling, Corsica was on the direct route to Japan, so we were both happy. Now when I hear or read the phrase 'Those who go down to the sea in ships see the wonders of the Lord' I think of Ed.

We left Cannes in late evening, that being the advice I had received in the bar where we met other sailors. The reason for this was that we would arrive off Corsica in daylight and I was told the first sight of land would be a mountain shaped like a wedge and that if I went to the right of this, Calvi would ultimately appear. With no tides to worry about and a good forecast, I laid off a course for Calvi and, having showed Ed the basics of steering a compass course, I turned in. As I was sleeping in a quarter berth he only had to rap his knuckles on the cockpit seat if he had any worries. It seemed as if I had barely put my head on my pillow when there was knocking by my head. 'What's the problem?' I asked. 'Nothing, but I think you will be interested,' was Ed's reply.

Being brought up as a yachtsman who considered that a man's time off watch was sacrosanct, I was a bit disgruntled as I pulled myself out of the quarter berth and into the cockpit where Ed pointed to the north and handed me the binoculars. There was an irregular line of sparkling white shapes shining in the darkness, and after I had gathered my wits together I realised I was seeing the sun shining on the snow fields of the Alps. They were all of 150 miles away and I realised with amazement that I was seeing daylight from the darkness of the night. Well worth being woken up for.

Later the next day the wedge-shaped mountain appeared in the right place and we ultimately dropped anchor in Calvi from where Ed went ashore and continued on his journey to the land of the rising sun. It was as I was exploring the surroundings of Calvi that I unexpectedly came across a small plaque let into a rock face informing me that it was here that Nelson lost his eye in the storming of the castle at Calvi. I was now crewless, as I had been for most of the trip. I did get the offer of a crew, however, but I refused. As we had approached Corsica, one of the first things we noticed were numerous parachutists. It was, and may still be, the base for the French Foreign Legion and there always seemed to be scores of them drifting down from the sky. Three legionnaires wanted to crew for me and, what is more, pay for the privilege, for they wanted to desert.

All this came out as their spokesman, an Englishman, struck up a conversation with me in a bar. It was a difficult thing, and for him dangerous: the first thing he asked me was that I didn't turn around and face him, for as he said, 'You cannot trust anyone.' I had already heard of the last two legionnaires who had made an unsuccessful attempt to desert. They had reached Sardinia and been handed back to the Legion by the Italian authorities. They had been discharged later as permanent cripples. Rumour had it that the Italians now had a less stringent attitude towards deserters and on this premise all the three men wanted was to be landed on the Italian mainland. Though sympathetic to their plight, there was too much at risk. The idea entered my head that once on board, with the three of them to me alone, they might not consider the Italian mainland far enough away. It was enough for me to finish my drink and get up and walk away.

Kath and the girls joined me at this point and we went into Ajaccio, the birthplace of Napoleon, France's most famous son. When we visited his actual

birthplace I found out that Napoleon was only just French, French by a day, for Corsica (which had been Italian) had been ceded to France the day before Napoleon was born.

From Ajaccio we started our circumnavigation of the island. It was a trip for which a boat was ideal. On board, once provisioned, we were completely independent. Many of the anchorages we used were deserted and some of them were idyllic. The Lavettzis in the Straits of Bonifacio fitted both descriptions. It was little more than a scattering of sunbaked rocks, some of which provided tenuous anchorages. So clear was the water we could see the anchor and chain on the sand beneath us. Invariably any French yachts that anchored

**Kath and Lodestone taken from Stone Point in the Walton Backwaters. This photo was used as a Yachting Monthly cover.**

PEYTON

**'I take it you didn't read that article "marinating for mariners"?'**

there left in the late afternoon for Bonifacio so that we had the place to ourselves. I had visited the Lavettzis before Kath had arrived, and shared an anchorage with a small British yacht. No doubt the skipper was annoyed to see me arrive, and it was his mast sticking out over the rocks that had told me there was an anchorage there and which had led me into it. Seeing the red ensign I rowed over. He was a singlehander from Lymington in a boat called *Paula* and the upshot was a memorable meal. Memorable not in exceptional gastronomic delights, though they were not lacking, but in the providing of it. On my accepting his invitation to stay for a meal he put on a pair of flippers, a face mask and, with a spear gun in his hand, he flopped over the side. In what to me seemed a very short time he was back on board with enough fish to make our dinner. I doubt if one could do that nowadays.

We spent almost six weeks, most of the school holiday, sailing around Corsica and exploring some of the Northern Sardinian coast. It was cruising as it should be. Everything, the crew, the cruising ground, the weather, the boat, seemed to combine for the best. The only snag we came up against was when we got back to Calvi. The forecast for our trip back to the mainland was not the best. However, we were well crewed, as a friend of ours, Vernon, had joined us. Vernon was a construction engineer, stolid and stocky, whom I had first met when he came on a charter weekend. We also had Patric. Patric was a English speaking Frenchman who was hitching a lift. He was charming and confident, even arrogant, and he was hitching because he had missed his plane. He actually pointed to it as it flew overhead, a small Cessna with his brother piloting it. To me he represented another crew member who would make the watches easier, especially as he said he had sailed a lot, so I decided he could work his passage. However, he took to a bunk as sick as a dog as soon as we got outside of Calvi and he stayed there until he stepped ashore at Cannes.

PEYTON

'Did you get the forecast, John? I missed it.'

**'Yes, that's it, taxi to the airport'**

My wife sometimes tells people that when the house was struck by light-ning I never woke up, but strike a match on the boat and he's up like a jack in the box. I never rise to this because I know people who sail appreciate the truth of this and the people who Kath tells the story to don't.

Nevertheless I had woken up, I was in the quarter berth, my usual berth at sea, and I could tell the boat was comfortable and going well. She had a beam wind and two reefs in the main and one in the head sail. I shone a torch around the cabin and everybody except Patric seemed to be asleep. Then I heard Hilary, who was on watch, laugh, and I realised that this was what had woken me up. I stuck my head through the hatch and asked her if she was all right. 'I'm all right,' she replied, 'but as you're up come and look at this' so I went into the cockpit. It was a magnificent moonlit night with clouds scudding across the sky and, as they shaded and revealed the moon, the sea was changing from shades of indigo to silver and back again. *Lodestone* was bounding along as if she was enjoying it all, and bounding close alongside her, as if in unison with her was a group of dolphins. It was

an amazing combination of movement and beauty, the moonlight, the sea, the dolphins, and I said something to that effect to which Hilary replied, 'Wait'. And as I watched and waited the smallest dolphin I have ever seen popped up and I laughed. I could see why Hilary had laughed. It was an involuntary reaction. We both still remember it.

Patric left us at Cannes and I thought we had seen the last of him – but I did not know Patric. He came back to see if we would like a trip in the family plane, a way of saying thank you, as he put it. For what reasons Kath and the girls turned this offer down I can no longer remember, but only Vernon and I accepted. My pleasant expectations of a sightseeing trip of the area soon went by the board. We quickly realised that Patric's sole ambition was to make us sick. His being sick on the trip back from Calvi had been a blow to his pride and he wanted to even things up. He did everything he could with that plane with always the sideways glance to see how we had reacted. We saw nothing of Cannes but we weren't sick and we never saw Patric again. Kath and the girls left us at Cannes and Vernon and I, now homeward bounders, sailed west.

It may seem strange but I was now getting a bit bored with the Med and looking forward to being in home waters. In later years Hilary, who sailed a lot in the Caribbean, told me they had a saying that was common when she was out there: 'Another bloody day in Paradise', and that summed up my feelings pretty well. But I'd got it out of my system and I'm glad I did it.

# Chapter 9

## Lodestone returns

The Canal du Midi was obviously the quickest route home and at Sète we had the problem of lowering the mast. On making inquiries as to how this could be done we were directed to a bar, the owner of which had a brother who had a mobile crane. I was quite willing to pay for this, but it was obvious that their idea of what was reasonable (they had the only crane) wasn't mine. It was seeing a sunken coaster in the harbour that allowed us to bypass them. We rowed out to the coaster and it was soon obvious that one of the davits would be ideal for our purpose. With a hammer to remove the rust and a drop of oil to get the sheave moving we lashed *Lodestone* alongside the sunken ship and, using the block on the davit, lowered *Lodestone*'s mast away. We went to the bar afterwards for a celebratory drink and I think the bar owner realised his monopoly was over for other people had seen our activities and I knew if one yachtsman had seen the potential of the davit the grapevine would see to it they all had.

The Canal du Midi was a fascinating section of the trip. The potential for linking the Atlantic to the Med had been first realised by the Romans but it was in the late 1600s that the French actually built it, all 300 miles plus. The fact that there was a sea at both ends also meant that it catered for seagoing boats of the time with a beam of over 14ft. The overall feeling of the Canal du Midi was that little had altered over the years. With its old towns and mature trees it was like stepping back in time. You realised the grooves in the walls of the locks had been scored there hundreds of years ago. It was almost imperceptible but as we headed northwest through the Midi, after weeks of being bare footed and wearing only shorts, we started resurrecting clothing and footwear that had been unused for months.

It was as we were going down the Gironde we had our last telling memory of France. We were passing an island whose name is fixed in my mind but where it is on the Gironde I have no idea. The island was the Ile de Verte and it was given over to vines. We tied up to a small jetty because we were running out of diesel and, as we could see a tractor among the vines, we hoped there was a chance we could buy a gallon or two of diesel. We landed and went up to the small house and were welcomed with open arms. The owner worked alone on the island: lonely and bored stiff, he was almost a castaway. Even the language barrier failed to damp his welcome so pleased was he to see another face. Glasses were put on the table and wine was poured in them more times than was sensible. He got over to us in sign language that he saw the occasional yacht passing but none stopped. We had to tell our friends (he assumed all yachtsmen knew each other) that they would always be welcome on the Ile de Verte.

When we finally left, our diesel tank was topped up and we were more than merry. We also had a number of bottles of the island's produce all labelled 'Ile de Verte' safely stowed away. We were still in this jolly mood when we saw the only yacht we met in the Gironde stemming the current on his way upstream. Immediately I opened the throttle and steered towards it. To the other skipper we were on a collision course and he opened his throttle and steered away from us. Our shouts and waves were to no avail, and as he had more power he quickly left us, obviously suspicious as to what we wanted. It is one of my most sincere regrets in this life that I didn't make a more favourable contact with that skipper as I have no doubt our host earlier in the day saw this yachtsman steam by without even glancing at the Ile de Verte.

Vernon's time was running out and as we reached the mouth of the Gironde I decided we would make use of what time I had left with a crew and get back to England as soon as possible. As chance was to have it, a good proportion of this trip was to provide some of the best sailing I have ever had.

We stocked up in Royan and cast off with about 400 miles to go. As I never kept a log I can't say what that first section was like, but after we passed Ushant it is fixed in my memory. We had an easterly wind, a fair beam wind for England, and anywhere in England would do. We were carrying everything when the wind freshened. I thought a reef was called for and I dropped the main to do this. It was as we were putting the reef in that I realised that *Lodestone* was sailing herself under headsail and mizzen. She was perfectly balanced and comfortable. Never one to look a gift horse in the mouth, I finished the reefing but never hoisted the mainsail and left her to herself. She continued to do this even when the wind increased, but as long as she kept on going so comfortably we neither touched the tiller nor altered the sheets.

Our watches were spent in the comfort of the doghouse. With all round visibility we never had to go into the cockpit and we never wore our oilskins. It was probably a hundred miles we covered in this manner and I have never had a sail remotely like it since. We might have been able to sail it faster but I doubt if we could have sailed it more comfortably. We picked up a mooring in Falmouth and the skipper of the yacht on the next moorings told me he had been waiting for three days for favourable conditions to do the crossing, which we had just done in comfort.

Vernon left me here and I started coast hopping my way east alone. Between Falmouth and the North Foreland I have one memory – it was of a good turn that was done to me. It happened off Bridport. I was anchored off waiting for enough water to enter and it was night. A shout brought me up on deck, a small fishing boat was close alongside and the fisherman, who had obviously worked out why I, a strange boat, was anchored there, asked me one question 'What's your draught?' I told him and he replied 'You'll be all right' and he disappeared into the narrow entrance. I pulled up my anchor and followed him in. A short time later as I crept cautiously into the harbour a voice told me where to lie and a dark figure took my lines, but my thanks fell, if not on deaf ears, on disappearing ears for he was gone. But never forgotten.

Rounding the North Foreland was like coming home. Perhaps the sun did not shine so much, perhaps the sea wasn't blue and clear but these were home waters, and they were appreciated all the more for my having sailed elsewhere.

*Lodestone* was to sail these waters winter and summer for the next ten years. To me, sailing out of the River Crouch seemed the ideal area for a charter boat. Once you are out of the Crouch there are 13 rivers to make for and explore, all possible in a weekend depending on the prevailing conditions. When conditions were ideal we could make Calais and back in a weekend and my regulars always had their passports in their bags on the offchance. Not that they were always necessary as often in those days the only Frenchman to come on board was the one taking your orders for your duty free allowance. And not only did he come on board to take your order but he delivered the order back to the boat as well. On week-long charters it was invariably France and Holland we went to and I could always get a crew for such junkets as 'Sail Amsterdam' or 'Brest 96'. Only now do I truly appreciate what a marvellous job it was. You had a crew of half a dozen enthusiastic dinghy sailors in a holiday mood and out for a week's enjoyment. You pointed them in the right direction and then hung on to the coat tails of their oilskins – and at the end of the week they paid you!

'Pity about the weather, Skip,
when we're all psyched up for a weekend's work'

What's more, they invariably tipped me and some came year after year for over thirty years, knowing that they provided me with the basis of many an article and innumerable cartoons. Of course there were occasions, say tying down a reef in the middle of the North Sea on a wet and windy night, when it was not immediately apparent that I had a good job, but on the whole job satisfaction summed it up.

The cartoons I was now selling to the English yachting magazines started generating work of their own. My cartoons started appearing in foreign magazines such as the German *Die Yacht* and the French *Voiles et Voiliers*. Because sailing was an international pastime all they had to do was translate the captions. Even the Japanese used them. I had a couple of weeks in America sailing in the Chesapeake Bay, an area about as big as the English Channel, to do a book of especially American cartoons.

However, it was some of the articles I either submitted or was commissioned to do that provided the most interest to me. One was with the early flotilla holidays in the Greek Islands. At that time, there were only three flotillas of ten boats each and the flotilla leaders had to ensure that they arrived in such ports as Levkas on alternate evenings so as not to overwhelm the facilities there. Now, of course, there is a huge marina and wall to wall restaurants. I can't get over how primitive it was when I was first sent there to write up a bareboat holiday. Seeing a flock of hens by a house, we anchored and rowed ashore to ask the man who was sitting outside if we could buy some eggs. As we approached he stood up, pulling up his trousers and buckling up his belt, and the hens moved in to clean up. A casual remark

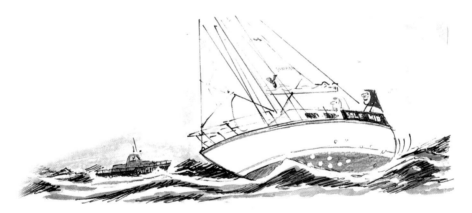

'See, we're not the only ones out'

to a English-speaking bar owner as to where we could buy a couple of lemons for our evening gin and tonic was passed on to the locals in his bar. It seemed as if it was only minutes before we were being offered lemons by the hundreds. We felt duty bound to buy a sackful. When buying potatoes we had to wait until they were dug up.

I have a strong visual picture of a Turkish village where the goings-on incensed the women of our party. We had gone ashore and in the village square there were about thirty rows of chairs and on inquiring we were told that on that evening a television set was to be put up in the village for the very first time. What incensed the women was that behind these rows of chairs there was a 10ft gap and then two rows of chairs for the women of the village.

'OK, sheet her in'

On another commission, I was fortunate to be sailing, in the true sense, aboard the sail training ship *Sir Winston Churchill* in the heaviest weather I have ever encountered at sea. It was March, the first trip of its season and I was on board to provide a photo feature of the voyage. The wind was a steady force ten touching eleven. We were dousing a foresail when the lookout shouted a warning, 'Here's a big one! Hang on!' as a sea came crashing on board. I grabbed the nearest thing at hand, which was one of the safety bars over the forward hatch. My nose was pressed against the glass as the seas cascaded over me and as the water ran off the hatch I realised I was looking down through the glass at a man asleep in his hammock. As I watched I saw his mouth open and his nose pucker and I realised he was snoring – yet barely a couple of feet away I was hanging on for my life in a world of howling wind and water.

Another trip came about when Mick the Brick asked me to serve as temporary mate on the motor barge he was working on. The skipper had been sent to jail and Mick had been promoted to skipper. The only person he could think of for a temporary mate at short notice was me. Barely an hour after receiving a phone call in the comforts of home I was standing on a lonely sea wall flashing a torch into the darkness towards a distant riding light as I waited for Mick to see it and scull ashore to pick me up.

Yet of all these varied boats I was happy to sail on I was incredibly lucky not to sail on one particular vessel. Kath came home one day saying she had met John Puxley in Burnham. John was the son of the man from whom I had bought *Vagrant*, my first boat, and he was crewing on a Burnham boat in the Fastnet. They were a crew member short – did I want the berth? Kath knew I had always wanted to do a Fastnet and more or less took up the offer on my behalf. But I refused – why I can no longer remember, for I seldom refused a sail. Perhaps a deadline for some job I was doing, a previous promise, but whatever it was I have no idea and I have racked my memory many a time since. The boat John was sailing was *Trophy*, the year was 1979, and she went down and John was drowned.

In the ten years I was chartering with *Lodestone* I made many good friends. I also had what I called failed charterers. These were charterers who never sailed with me again, though I often sailed with them. They were the charterers who took to sailing to such an extent that they bought or built their own boat.

And with the 'normal' charterers I had many pleasant times, sometimes away from sailing. With one Swiss charterer I often went skiing and because of this another friend, Danny, offered to do any jobs that needed doing on *Lodestone* when I was away skiing and *Lodestone* was laid up. It became a tradition for a few years that Danny and I would sail *Lodestone* up to Wintringham Haven on the River Humber starting on Boxing Day. Danny, who had first come on a weekend charter, had been in the same Division as I had been in during the war so we had a lot in common. He sailed with me a lot after our first meeting, generally as mate. He was impervious to seasickness, handy with his hands, good with engines, and with a laid back character he was an asset on any boat. We sailed around England together – and I would advise you if you do it to go around clockwise. The route allowed family, friends and charterers to join us in various places and it is a trip I would recommend to any yachtsman.

# Chapter 10

## Brimstone

It was after I had been chartering *Lodestone* for about seven years that, perhaps with delusions of grandeur, I built another boat. Or at least built the hull. Also designed by Alan Hill, she was built in ferro and was 35ft long, a yawl rigged centreboarder – she was in many respects a smaller *Lodestone*. She had two ideas that were original – one that I now realise was unnecessary and one that I wish I had on my present boat. With regards to the former, *Morning Cloud*, the boat of the Prime Minister of the day, had just sunk in bad weather off Selsey Bill. Part of the blame for this was that as the boat suffered a knock-down, the washboards, which had a slight angle on them, only had to move a few inches before they fell out. The outcome was obvious and the sea flooded in. With this fresh in my mind my idea for *Brimstone* was not to have any washboards at all. To go below you eased yourself up on what was to all effects a pulpit around the hatch, then lowered yourself below. It was obviously safer but inconvenient. The wash boards on my present boat are removable.

The other idea was used successfully on *Brimstone* and I now regret not using it on my present boat *Touchstone*. Once the ferro hull was built the builders invariably finished it in wood. A beam shelf (or wedge) was fitted on a right angled ferro shelf to take the deck beams and deck. My idea was that the top of the hull should be curved over (ferro construction lends itself to curves) to match and support the cambered deck. What was lost in deck

area was compensated for in building simplicity and strength.

Together the two boats, *Lodestone* and *Brimstone,* cruised the Thames estuary. We went ashore, as the saying goes, mob handed and landlords were glad to see us. But I realised I had made a mistake in the conception of chartering with two boats. My idea that sailing with two boats would double the pleasure was a fallacy. Besides the extra maintenance of another boat, the vagaries of the weather was another drawback and soon made itself

**Brimstone from Lodestone. They sailed many miles in company.**

obvious. There were times when, because of an inexperienced crew, a reliable skipper was needed on *Brimstone.* Yet you never knew when one would be needed or whether you could get one, generally at short notice. Added to this was the fact that so much was out of my control, often being out of sight over the horizon. The realisation that I was no businessman and the extra work, which included book work, needed to keep another boat sea worthy, made me put *Brimstone* up for sale. She sold almost overnight and life continued as before taking out charterers on *Lodestone.*

Both *Lodestone* and *Brimstone* were basic boats with built-in work to keep the crew occupied. There were no winches either on the mast or for anchor or headsails. No echo sounder – someone was almost always swinging the lead – and a hand-start engine. On *Lodestone* I had a starting handle which three men could grasp at the same time, though in an emergency when the adrenaline was flowing I could start it on my own. As for *Brimstone* herself, though I sailed miles with her, I was seldom on board.

One trip in particular I do recollect. The two boats were sailing in company and we were reaching down the Swin with a light wind and a fair tide. The Barrow Sand was covered in basking seals. As I was always thinking of ways to keep the crew occupied, the seals gave me an idea. One of the party had his guitar with him and as I had heard that seals were susceptible to music I decided to give it a trial.

We ran both boats aground on the sand knowing that the making tide

would soon lift us off. The guitarist sat strumming away on the forehatch while we all sat silently in the cockpits and watched and waited. After a while three seals swam out towards us to investigate, but then the tide lifted the boats and swept them away before the experiment could be properly concluded. We never found out whether all seals were music lovers, or just those three. But it was successful enough to suggest that further research would be interesting.

Shortly afterwards, still working on my principle of keeping the crews occupied, I decided to do something I had often thought of doing when the conditions were right, and they were at that moment. This was to climb up onto the Red Sand Tower, one of the towers that had been built in the estuary during the war as a platform for anti-aircraft guns. The dinghy on *Lodestone* was first away. I found it difficult to row up close as the towers were built on huge concrete blocks and the tide is constricted as it runs between them. There were strong currents and turbulence, but finally I was close enough to make a grab for a rung of the ladder. I got a shock as the rung crumbled away in my hand to the thickness of a pencil. Over 50 years of wind and weather and a salt laden atmosphere had taken its toll. If I had had any sense I would have let go and gone back to the boat.

Why I still decided to climb up it I put down to stupidity. We – for I only had one companion, one of my regulars from Frampton Sailing Club in Gloucester – climbed the ladder using the side of the rungs. Once on the spidery walkways it was like leaving footprints in snow except the footprints we were leaving were in rust. But the unusual view of the estuary with the two boats backing and filling below I will always remember. Exploring the living quarters, we found evocative graffiti scrawled on the walls. 'Roll on 88', for the demob system was numbered: the first to be conscripted were the first to be demobilised. Demob numbers loomed large in a soldier's life. Some five miles from land, this must have been a bleak and lonely posting, in some cases, I understand, leading to suicide.

Our return trip to the dinghy was just as perilous. Looking down with trepidation at the dinghy at least 40ft below, and knowing the state of the ladder, it came home to me that life is sweet. As it was, we survived to sail another day. Like many things in life one shouldn't have done it, but I was glad I had. I have sailed past Red Sand Tower and its fellows many times since that day and have always been surprised that they are still standing.

# Chapter 11

## Touchstone

It was obvious that my last boat *Touchstone* had to be built in ferro because only in ferro could my ideas be incorporated. She is 38ft x 11ft x 3ft with two drop boards that give her a draught of 7ft. Her ballast is also the cabin sole which is four inches of reinforced concrete, and the skin of the hull itself tapers to just over half an inch at deck level. The slots for the boards to slide in went from deck level to just below the water level. The boards themselves were an aerofoil section and because only one was down at a time it allowed them to be toed in five degrees to help her up to weather.

Most yachtsmen have realised at some time or another, generally in light winds, that the mast could carry more canvas. In fact, many hotshot boats have battens at the head of their mainsails, which is to all intents and purposes a small gaff. It gives more area where the normal main is least efficient and the winds are stronger. As the owner of a relatively heavy displacement boat (seven and a half tonnes) I have always been conscious of this, so the idea of a gaff sail with a top sail appealed, it would almost double the sail area of the Bermudian and, when necessary, I could always reef. This is made easy because everything – topsail, mainsail and the slide which takes the place of the gaff jaws – runs in the same mast track. Everything goes up on one halyard. A vang running from the end of the gaff to the top of the mizzen mast was also fitted so that the gaff itself did not sag off and could be trimmed accordingly. She was an efficient boat, though – as planned – labour intensive as the drop boards had to be hauled up or let down on each tack.

In the 26 years I sailed *Touchstone* we had our ups and downs. Nothing serious occurred, but two incidents do come to mind. The first was when the centreboard dropped out in Bray harbour on Alderney. There were two of us

**Touchstone with one reef in. The topsail never comes off, and all reefing is done in the mainsail.**

on board and it took us some time to find it, with one of us rowing the dinghy and the other looking under the water through a facemask, even though the first thing I did when I heard it go was to jump to the hatch and take compass bearings of our position. We were then fortunate enough to pressgang someone in the area who was wearing goggles and a wetsuit. He obligingly dived down and made a line fast to the board. It was quite heavy; 9ft long and an inch thick of metal. We then towed it to the beach at high water and took the ground alongside. All we had to do then, or so we thought, was to dig a hole in the sand under the boat and manhandle the boat back into its slot.

A trip up to St Anne's to buy a shovel, then, with an audience of curious holidaymakers, we set to work. What happened was that the hole got about 2ft deep but no deeper: as it went longer and wider, the sides of the hole fell in and it filled with sandy slurry. The remark of my companion, up to his knees in slurry with eight tonnes of boat looming over him, put into words the obvious: 'You know, Mike, a works inspector wouldn't pass this.'

Eventually, seeing the hopelessness of the task, our ever-growing audience of spectators willingly hauled the board to a stone jetty where, when the height of the jetty and *Touchstone*'s deck coincided, we slid the board on deck and it came back to Burnham as deck cargo. Although this incident could have been disastrous if the boat had moved while the digging was going on, the next could have been the same, only quicker.

It was winter and I was sailing with five friends, every one a yacht owner, yachtmasters all. We were motoring up the River Colne and as we were passing the entrance to Roman River (a short, twisty, and drying creek) someone asked if we could go up it. As the tide was high and I had been up it before without incident, I replied 'Yes'. I was below at the time and I remember it well. I was poking the fire when I felt the motion of the boat falter. My initial thought was that she had gone aground. As I pushed my head out of the hatch the top third of the mast came down: we had struck an overhead electricity cable and it had burnt through the alloy mast. We were lucky no one had been holding a shroud and that no other damage or injury was incurred.

It was later as I was attempting to reinsure *Touchstone* that I got a real shock. They refused to insure me. When I asked why I was told that if a claim went over a certain amount they never reinsured.

'But it only cost £900 to re-sleeve the mast and I haven't made a claim for over twenty years.'

Back came the reply, 'Your mast was the least of our worries. There were claims from a computer centre, an industrial estate, a shopping mall...' etc, etc. He continued, 'And as a matter of interest I worked on that other claim. I even remember the name of the boat. It was *Sugar Creek*. And I remember it because it was the first job I worked on when I started in insurance 26 years ago.'

*Touchstone* was launched in 1981 and for 26 years has shuttled about between the Wash and the North Foreland, winter and summer, in fair weather or foul.

As Kipling put it,

God gave man all earth to love
But since man's heart is small
Ordained that one spot should prove
Beloved over all

I consider myself fortunate that the east coast is where I ended up. Last year my publisher suggested I write it down before I lost my marbles, and this is it. I have no complaints.